TROLL MILLER ATCHLEY

FAMILIES IN LATER LIFE

Families in Later Life

Lifetime Series in Aging

Available now from Wadsworth:

Available now from Brooks/Cole:

Available now from Duxbury:

Forthcoming titles from Wadsworth:

Families in Later Life

Lillian E. Troll
Rutgers University

Sheila J. Miller
Scripps Foundation Gerontology Center, Miami University,
Ohio

Robert C. Atchley
Scripps Foundation Gerontology Center, Miami University,
Ohio

Wadsworth Publishing Company, Inc.
Belmont, California

Sociology and Gerontology Editor: Stephen Rutter
Cover Designer: Joe di Chiarro
Production Editor: Sandra Craig

Printed in the United States of America

1 2 3 4 5 6 7 8 9 10—83 82 81 80 79

Library of Congress Cataloging in Publication Data
Troll, Lillian E.
        Families in later life.

        Bibliography:
        Includes index.
        1. Family—United   States.   2.   Aged—United   States—
Family relations.   I.   Miller, Sheila J., joint author.
II.   Atchley, Robert C., joint author.   III.   Title.
HQ536.T67   301.42'0973   78–21913
ISBN 0–534–00613–2

Preface

One day in 1969, Lillian Troll got a call from Bernice Neugarten, who had been asked by Carlfred Broderick to write a review of the literature on the family of later life for a special edition of the *Journal of Marriage and the Family*. Bernice Neugarten asked Lillian to coauthor this review because she was overcommitted but felt that the job was important. Since the area was one of special interest to Lillian, she accepted the invitation. Over most of the next year, Lillian made several extended visits to Bernice in Chicago to discuss the project. Thus, the review was really a joint product, enriched by the fertile input of Bernice even though she later decided that she should not be designated a coauthor. This review, which appeared in the second number of the 1971 issue of the *Journal of Marriage and the Family,* was reprinted later that year as part of the National Council of Family Relations monograph called *A Decade of Family Research and Action,* edited by Carlfred Broderick. It was introduced to readers in two previously separated fields—studies of the family and gerontology— and apparently made each field aware of the other, leading to infiltration of theory and research information in both directions. In fact, some of the research in the 1970s that is cited in this volume seems to be showing the effect of this cross-fertilization.

In September 1975, Sheila Miller asked Lillian Troll to join her in expanding the original decade review into a textbook, bringing the literature coverage up to date in the process. This project did not get under way for two more years, however, by which time Robert Atchley had been added to the team. Thus, the present volume has evolved from the work and ideas of several people. Since each of the three authors has an individual viewpoint as well as a separate academic discipline, there were times of marked disagreement. Fortunately, these disagreements were all resolved into what we believe are meaningful syntheses.

Because we represent the disciplines of psychology, sociology, and family studies, we have been able to draw from theory and research in all three areas, and we trust that our book will find a wider use than a book based on any one discipline. The study of the families of later life is truly a multidisciplinary topic. We want to note that the authors are listed in inverted alphabetical order, which should not be interpreted as signifying significance of contributions. Material has been drawn not only from the *Decade Review* cited in the first paragraph, but also from *Early and Middle Adulthood* by Lillian E. Troll, published by Brooks/Cole Publishing Company in Monterey, California, 1975, and from *Social Forces in Later Life* by Robert Atchley, published by Wadsworth Publishing Company, 1972 and 1977.

We deliberately chose the title *Families* instead of *Family* because we believe that it is important to understand the variation in family structure, in family relationships, and in family life that exists in the United States at this time. Fortunately, we decided to limit our coverage to this country; otherwise we would have had to give even more stress to variations. There is no specific chapter titled ''Variations,'' but we try to point them out at each point in the book. Among the more significant sources of variation, as we indicate throughout, are traditionalism versus expressionism; sex; generation or cohort; urban versus rural; social class; and ethnicity, for example, black versus white. These sources of variation often overlap; for instance, many black-white differences can be explained by social class and maybe by the value of family traditionalism. However, there are also other sources of variation, and these are mentioned when appropriate.

Throughout this book we ask many questions about families in later life for which there are no research data as yet. We hope that we can stimulate research that focuses on such questions.

Finally, we added Chapter 8, ''Implications,'' because even at this early stage of research, we can make certain statements that would be useful to the general public, to policy makers, and to practitioners. This last chapter is brief and suggestive rather than comprehensive. It is meant to alert rather than to advise, to turn theory and practice in more informed directions.

We want to thank our own families and our friends who shared with us experiences about their own families. They have been not only patient and supportive but also inspirational. We want to thank Carlfred Broderick and Bernice Neugarten for starting this project. We also want to thank Stephen Rutter of Wadsworth for riding herd on us during the ups and downs of writing, discussing, and revising. And we want to thank the reviewers—Sylvia Clavan, St. Joseph's College; Gary D. Hansen, Brigham Young University; and Sally Van Zandt, University of Nebraska—and the editors and typists who helped us prepare the manuscript.

Lillian Troll
Sheila Miller
Robert Atchley

Contents

Chapter One

Introduction

Family Literature and Later Life

Even though most of us spend our lives within family groups, textbooks on the family tend to focus on the events of early life, the creation and development of new husband/wife units, and early child-rearing experiences. In the course of a lifetime, most of us play a variety of family roles—child, spouse, parent, grandparent, sibling, cousin, or in-law. Textbooks have a lot to say about mate selection, about marital adjustment in the early years of marriage, about parenting of young children, and about sibling rivalry among children, but they have very little to say about dating and remarriage past adolescence, about marital satisfaction in middle or old age, about the relations between older parents and their adult children, or about sibling relationships among adults. Recent family texts are beginning to include material on these subjects, but the coverage is still scanty.

Families in Later Life is designed to fill this gap, to deal with the familial lives of older Americans, including those who have never married or never become parents.

Writing about families in later life has, until recently, been the province of two relatively unrelated groups of social scientists: those primarily concerned with family issues, and those concerned with aging men and women. Some of the major theoretical and empirical studies in each area are just beginning to be recognized by the other area. With this growing permeation, we can begin to look for sophisticated syntheses and a new understanding of the full range of family relationships.

Function and Plan of This Book

This book can serve several purposes. It can be used by students and teachers to augment general family texts. It can be used by counselors working with families in later life. It can be used by researchers to identify topics in need of further research. For all of these prospective readers, we have tried to provide an overview of theory and research, to synthesize and review the existing literature, to identify research issues and needs, and to point out some implications of this information for counselors, teachers, and researchers. But most of all, this book is for people who are members of families, to help them understand their own families better.

Families in Later Life is organized around the variety of family relationships. Before discussing specific family relationships, however, in Chapter 2 we cover the issues, perspectives, and problems that provide useful theoretical and practical background for the chapters to follow. The issues raised include controversies within family studies over whether isolated, nuclear, or modified extended families are most common in America; whether family ties are merely a means to an end or an end in themselves; and whether the unit of study should be the individual, the married couple, or the family system. Perspectives include developmental, family life-cycle, interactional, and generational approaches to theories of family dynamics. Problems discussed include cultural norms and stereotypes that cloud our ability to see what families can or should be; intervening variables such as financial status, health, and longevity that also complicate the problems of studying families in later life; and, finally, a discussion of some of the methodological problems that have confronted researchers. Readers who are only slightly interested in these issues may want to skim this chapter at first and return to it when the rest of the book has been read.

Chapter 3 is about older couples. It covers the prevalence of marriage among older adults; the lengthening of the "empty nest" period of marriage; social class and ethnic variations among older couples; economic and health factors affecting older couples; marital satisfaction and factors influencing it; household division of labor; sexuality; retirement; divorce; and remarriage. Obviously, this chapter covers a lot of ground. Unlike the other chapters, which have a single chapter summary, Chapter 3 has summaries at the end of each of its major sections.

Chapter 4 is about being unmarried in later life. It begins with the prevalence of widowhood, the meaning of bereavement, and the consequences of widowhood for both men and women, including long-term versus short-term consequences. It then looks at the prevalence of divorce among older adults and sexuality among the widowed and divorced. Finally, it considers implications of having never married.

Chapter 5 is about parents and their adult children. It begins with a look at the prevalence of adult children among older people. It then considers family structure and dynamics from a number of perspectives: residential proximity, interaction frequency, mutual aid, and family values. Following this is a review of the *quality* of relationships between parents and their adult children in terms of both intergenerational continuity and feelings about one another. The discussion then moves to duty as a factor in parent/adult-child relationships and the issue of whether feelings or a sense of duty most influence them. Following a discussion of how sex, social class, and geographic or social mobility influence parent/adult-child relationships, the chapter ends by discussing how parent/adult-child relationships change over the life course. Some important sources of change include retirement, widowhood, health, and finances.

Chapter 6 is about being a grandparent or great-grandparent. It begins by discussing the prevalence of grandchildren among older adults, then moves to grandchildren's perceptions of their grandparents, interaction of grandparents with grandchildren, and grandparents' perceptions of grandchildren. It then considers the nature of the grandparent/grandchild relationship. The chapter ends with a brief discussion of great-grandparenthood.

Chapter 7 is about older people's relationships with siblings and other kin. It covers the prevalence of siblings among older adults, the nature of sibling relationships, and relations with extended kin and in-laws.

Chapter 8 deals with implications for the general public, for counseling or psychotherapy, and for the academic community.

Definitions

What do we mean by *families in later life?* Some students of the family would only apply the term *family* to a childrearing couple and their offspring. In this view, once the children are grown and have gone from the household, the *family of orientation* is disbanded or is diminished to the residual couple; when one member of that couple dies, that family presumably ceases to exist. But research on older people

has challenged this view. According to nearly all gerontological surveys, older people are not isolated from their children. The children
have not truly gone. It seems appropriate to call the connections between parents, children, and grandchildren of all ages *families*.
Whether we want to use such terms as *extended families* or *modified
extended families* is a secondary issue, which we will discuss in the
next chapter.

Later life in a family context cannot be reliably translated into
chronological ages. It is more meaningful to use references based on
family status. Most of the discussion in this book refers to the post-
childrearing family. Some post-childrearing parents are only in their
thirties; others do not reach this point until their fifties. In this book,
however, we concentrate on people past their forties because those are
the ages most studies have chosen to focus upon.

That husband/wife childrearing families are popularly seen as
the only true families is easily illustrated. Ten years ago, a student
about age thirty came to Lillian Troll for help with her term paper for a
course on the family. "You see," she said, "I don't know anything
about families because I am not married." "But you grew up in a
family, didn't you?" she was asked. "Oh yes, of course," she said.
"And you still see your parents and other relatives?" "Oh yes, frequently. But I thought a family had to be a husband and wife who were
raising children."

In a seminar Professor Troll taught on the family, students
were asked to rate their feelings of closeness to members of their
family. Again, the limited nature of the students' definitions was clear.
They didn't think they could fulfill the assignment because, after all,
they were now no longer part of any family. They had left their family
of orientation and had not yet started their family of procreation. Also,
when they were asked to begin by listing all the relatives they knew
they had, they said that they hardly knew any. But at the next class
meeting, a week later, each of them sheepishly folded out large stapled
sheets with elaborate family trees. They couldn't believe they knew so
many relatives so well, and they also found that they had very strong
feelings about most of them—sometimes positive, sometimes negative.
They rarely felt neutral toward people in their family even though
many of their family members lived far away and were seen in-
frequently.

A third story: Professor Troll once ran a workshop designed to
train church members to direct family activities in their local churches.
The participants began by identifying themselves. As they went around

the table—there were about thirty people present—it was clear that everybody was verifying his or her family credentials. They were doing this by listing their marital condition—all were married—and by announcing the number, ages, and sexes of their children. When it was Professor Troll's turn, she said it was strange that no one had mentioned being the child of their parents. "Aha!" they all said, as if a door had opened, and then they quickly went around again talking about their parents and their grandparents. They had been given permission to include these older relatives as family. The workshop then began to focus on all generations and ended with a resolution to integrate all ages in church family activities.

Importance of Family in Later Life

One of the themes of this book is that families are alive and well; they are not dying or dead. They can influence the lives of most members of our society, from young children to old great-grandparents. In fact, where family relationships are too scanty or too distant, many people even create substitute or pseudo-families.

Families today can include same-sexed and opposite-sexed cohabiting partners, children of previous marriages (or of more informal pairings), as well as more "legitimate" great-grandparents, great-nephews, and cousins. Even though household units tend to remain nuclear in structure, interconnections among households are strong. Older people in our population, with the possible exception of orphans, are isolated from families only if they want to be or only when they are so deteriorated that they are no longer functioning social individuals.

One of the new issues in the study of families is the quality of human relationships. The study of families can be directed to such variables as frequency of contact among relatives, mutual obligations and helping patterns, and the bonds and feelings between people. These same variables apply to the study of other primary relationships. We may never reach an important understanding of family relationships until we study these variables and compare family relationships with friendships, particularly those that endure over long periods of time.

One of the most salient gerontological theories of the past two decades has been *disengagement theory,* which will be discussed in more detail later. Essentially, it tries to explain the tendency of many older people to withdraw from activities in the world around them. One

finding pertinent to this theory is clear, however. Older people sometimes disengage from their roles outside their families, but they rarely
disengage from their involvements inside their families. They disengage *into* rather than *from* their families. As their worlds shrink, their
spouses, children and grandchildren, and even their siblings and other
relatives become more important to them.

Table 1.1 shows the percent of the national study by Harris and
Associates (1975) of adults who have living relatives of various types
and how often they interact with these relatives. It is clear that the vast
majority of older Americans have living relatives of many kinds and are
in contact with them frequently. This is particularly true of older parents' contacts with adult children and grandchildren.

Most social life at all ages, including those of supposedly disengaging people, is with friends; 91 percent of people over sixty-five

Table 1.1. Contact with Friends and Family (Base: Have friends/relatives)

		When Last Seen (percent)			
Percent of Population Having Friends or Relatives	Within Last Day or So (Including Live With)	Within Last Week or Two	A Month Ago	Two to Three Months Ago	Longer Ago than That
Close Friends					
Public 18 to 64	97	64	30	3	1	2
Public 65 and over	94	60	31	5	2	2
Children					
Public 18 to 64	73	87	8	2	1	2
Public 65 and over	81	55	26	8	3	8
Brothers and Sisters					
Public 18 to 64	91	31	31	12	6	20
Public 65 and over	79	22	22	15	10	31
Parents					
Public 18 to 64	70	48	24	9	5	14
Public 65 and over	4	32	23	8	11	26
Grandchildren					
Public 65 and over	75	46	28	10	5	11
Grandparents					
Public 18 to 64	30	24	20	18	8	30

Source: From *The Myth and Reality of Aging in America,* a study prepared by
Louis Harris and Associates, Inc., for The National Council on the Aging,
Inc., Washington, D.C., © 1975. Used by permission.

who have friends (and 94 percent of them *do* have friends) see these friends almost every day. This percentage is not significantly lower than the 94 percent of younger people who see their friends all the time. Contact with children is almost as high. Three-fourths of all adults have living children, and even more persons over sixty-five do. The majority have seen their children within the last day or so. Of those who are parents, 95 percent under sixty-five see their children weekly (and many of these are post-childrearing) and 81 percent over sixty-five do. Considering the fact that very old parents may have problems with mobility, and also considering that these figures do not include letter writing and telephoning, there is abundant evidence that families exist in later life.

Chapter Two

Issues, Perspectives, and Problems

Chapter 1 tells you why we wrote this book and what we are including in it. The present chapter points out some issues in the field of families in later life, the variety of points of view that underlies existing thinking in this area, and some of the research and interpretation problems. Since this chapter is more abstract than most of the others and thus may require greater concentration, it could be harder for beginning students, many of whom may prefer to skim rather than to try to absorb all the material. In fact, some may choose to read this chapter last rather than at the beginning. We prefer to place it at the beginning because the points we make here underlie most of the material presented in later chapters; more advanced students should read the material presented here as a foundation for later chapters.

Issues

In Chapter 1 we alluded to several issues now in the forefront of discussions of families of later life. Such issues represent important questions around which current research is centered or to which new research should be directed. Here is a list of some of these issues or questions.

Nuclear Versus Extended Families

Most popular theories about families state that at an earlier point in our history, people lived in extended families that included under the same roof several generations and numerous collateral relatives. These theories state that now most people, if they belong to families at all, belong only to isolated nuclear-family units. Such *isolated nuclear families* are usually defined as husband/wife couples and their immature children who reside with them. Older people are seen as being isolated from their own grown children, from their parents, their siblings, and from all other relatives. A variety of social consequences have been attributed to this presumed shift in family structure. Among these are the problems of neglected old people and young children, as well as individual *anomie* or loneliness.

Such assumptions about isolation began to be challenged by large-scale surveys of older people conducted in the mid-1950s. These and more recent surveys all tend to show that an overwhelming proportion of people over sixty-five live near at least one child and that constant interchange of visits and help between older parents and their children is the rule rather than the exception. It is true that few lineal families actually live in the same household, but most gerontologists, on the basis of these repeated investigations (e.g., Sussman and Burchinal, 1962a, b; Litwak, 1960a, b; Adams, 1968a; Hill et al., 1970; Shanas et al., 1968; Cumming and Henry, 1961) now conclude that the nuclear family is not isolated from kin (see review by Troll, 1971a). Now, most family theorists speak of a *modified extended-family structure*.

It is true that not all gerontological family theorists agree with this conclusion. Some continue to emphasize the essential or functional isolation of older Americans as well as childrearing families (e.g., Smelser, 1966; Parsons, 1965; Gibson, 1972; Rosow, 1965b; Claven and Vatter, 1972). Even if we accept the "modified extended" conclusion, the question remains, however, how much older people are *involved* in these networks. Some researchers claim that the conjugal pair is the central focus of family life in American society, and that it makes little sense to examine relationships that are very far removed from the isolated family of procreation (Gibson, 1972). Some have even noted that associations with close friends and neighbors are more closely related to the morale of older people than are associations with their children (Arling, 1976). According to this view, a book such as ours would be based upon a fallacy. Others contend that *extended family systems* are the most typical and functional. These extended systems are seen as complicated networks tying members together both within and across generations. At this point, the evidence seems to weigh more heavily on the side of a "modified extended" family system, at least for lineal descendants or ascendants.

One problem with our present information is that it is all cross-sectional. In order to assess peoples' long-term involvement with kin we need longitudinal studies that follow family interactions over the years of life—controlled, of course, for such factors as sex, marital status, and kin availability. It would be important also to compare such data with life variations in involvement with intimate friends.

Nature of Family Ties: Instrumental Versus Intimate

When we begin with the assumptions that nuclear family units are interconnected and that at least parents and their children remain closely linked throughout life, we are led to the next question of *how* they are connected. One set of answers is that such connections are primarily *instrumental,* for extrinsic rather than intrinsic purposes. For example, relatives might help each other in order to keep up a network of mutual obligations to serve each of them in time of need. Or, by the same logic, such interchanges might be motivated by fear of social disapproval: that family members would face shame from other people around them if they did not live up to social rules about kin obligations. In fact, it is based upon this explanation that some theorists believe the kinship system is now disappearing, since urban industrialization is dissipating the power of such traditional norms and social pressures. Two other instrumental views derive from clinical psychopathological explanations. One is that family members who devote much of their lives to the care of other family members (such as many wives and mothers) are either getting satisfaction from martyrdom or have been unfortunately socialized to affiliative caring orientations—or both. Another instrumental explanation is that attention to, and concern about, other family members is motivated by feelings of guilt—and, in fact, may be neurotic and not in the best interests of either givers or receivers.

A varying set of answers is that such family connections are *intimate bonds* or attachments among people who have been closely involved over a long period of time—or whose involvement stems from particular critical periods in life, such as infancy or beginning parenthood. This kind of answer assumes that family members who are connected to each other in this way have a unique importance for each other and strong feelings, whether positive (love) or negative (hate).

Rather than regarding family ties as based upon the anticipated consequences of interaction, this view assumes that relatives find it *necessary* to interact, that there is intrinsic meaning to their interrelationships.

So far, this issue remains in the realm of speculation. We do
not have the kind of information we would need to do any more than
hypothesize. There are hopeful signs of new research on qualitative,
not only quantitative, interrelationships among family members, and in
the future we may be able to venture more conclusive statements. It
could very well be, of course, that because they are so complex, family
relationships are never unitary in motivation but combine several or all
of these reasons. More discussion of this theme appears in later chapters.

Stability Versus Change

Because most family research has been *cross-sectional,* done
at one point in time, many family theorists confine their attention to the
description or analysis of family behavior or structure of family roles at
one point in time. Even those whose orientation is from a *family development* perspective (see Part II of this chapter) may describe a
series of *stages* without attending to the transitions from one such state
to the next. A true developmental perspective, however, focuses on
the changes that occur over the family life course, the life paths of
different kinds of families, and even concomitants of the particular
kinds of life courses. Which antecedents predict life-long involvement
and which predict termination?

Another consequence of one-time research is the tendency to
assume that what is reported or seen at one moment is representative
of all moments. This is most applicable to the study of feelings. Husbands may feel very warm and loving in the morning and neutral or
hostile in the evening—or vice versa. Children may feel very close to
their aging parents at the time of an anniversary but a day later may
experience only the burdens of responsibility and obligations. Brothers
or sisters may arouse a warm glow of nostalgia and renewed affection
during a Thanksgiving dinner that will be virtually forgotten by
Christmas. As a later chapter will explore, family relationships probably ebb and flow—sometimes in large waves, sometimes in quickly
changing patterns.

Crises Versus Continuous
Development

Arising from the issue of stability versus change is the matter of the pattern and causations of change. Once we recognize the existence of changes in family life courses, we have to try to explain how and why they come about. Some family theorists see changes as primarily *continuous;* others postulate a *series of critical events* that lead to dramatic shifts in role constellations and relationships. In part, such differences can be traced to the family units and parameters focused upon. Investigators of marital satisfaction, for example, are more likely to perceive a continuous pattern, or at most a bimodal one. This might be even more true of investigators of parents' love for a child. On the other hand, investigators of role constellations or other family structure parameters may tend to uncover markedly discontinuous patterns.

Discontinuity is generally attributed to such major life events as marriage, death, birth, the empty nest, and divorce. Death of a parent or spouse can immediately alter all role constellations. Divorce can effect much the same drastic change. Birth may not change structure as much or at least as quickly, and a number of studies suggest that the departure of children from the home is also a more gradual process, perhaps the most gradual of all.

Generation Gap Versus Family
Solidarity

A recurrent theme in family research and theory is generational similarities and differences: *generational relationships*. While this issue has received most attention for hypothesized cleavages between youth and their middle-aged parents, it is equally relevant to generational boundaries in later life. Does the fact that parents and children—of any ages—are at different points in their own life development, as well as the fact that they are separated by positions and role relationships in the family and were born and socialized under differing historical circumstances, result in inevitable separation and, according to some theorists, even inevitable conflict? After reviewing the literature, Troll and Bengtson (1978) conclude that while individual developmental and historical effects are evident in values, opinions, and attitudes in a number of areas, cross-generational consensus within families is still apparent and it is likely that even offspring who may deviate markedly from their parents in generational *keynote* characteristics may still be carrying out the family theme. Above all, whether there is agreement or not on political orientations or lifestyle characteristics, close bonds tend to persist. This issue will be discussed in Chapter 5.

Social Change

Contemporary changes have influenced the *constellation of roles* and the *generational rhythm* within the family. To begin with, a decline in mortality rates since 1900 has added a fourth generation to many families; the positions of great-grandparent, great-aunt, and so on have become more evident. Moreover, as parents' age at birth of their last child declines, there is a shorter period between generations. In fifty years, this has declined from about thirty to about twenty years. This factor, along with increased life expectancy, has also increased the number of generations in a family.

Finally, a decline in birth rates has influenced the structure of the family. In 1910, the average couple had produced 4.5 children; by 1970, this number was 2.6. Thus, there were fewer family members *within each generation*. Although the overall trend has been one of decline, it has not been even. Birth rates have fluctuated a good bit since 1900. This means that we can expect future cohorts entering later life to vary widely in the average numbers of siblings, cousins, aunts, and uncles.

The rhythm of development within the family has altered over the last few generations. More people today live out their full life span, more parents limit the number of their children, and economic affluence permits young couples to get married before they are economically independent. The grandparents of today's young adults, who married in the first decade of the twentieth century, were married longer than the next two generations before they had their first child. However, they had children at closer intervals and continued having children for a longer period of time (see Table 2.1). Today's middle-aged generation got married during the Depression and had to delay having children. Of the three generations studied by Hill and his associates (1970), the grandparents spent the most years raising children. Table 2.1 shows the earlier progression in age of first marriage between 1890 and 1960. In 1890, women married at twenty-two, on the average, and men at twenty-six. In 1960, brides were twenty and grooms twenty-two.

Table 2.1.   Profile of the Timing of Family Composition by Generation

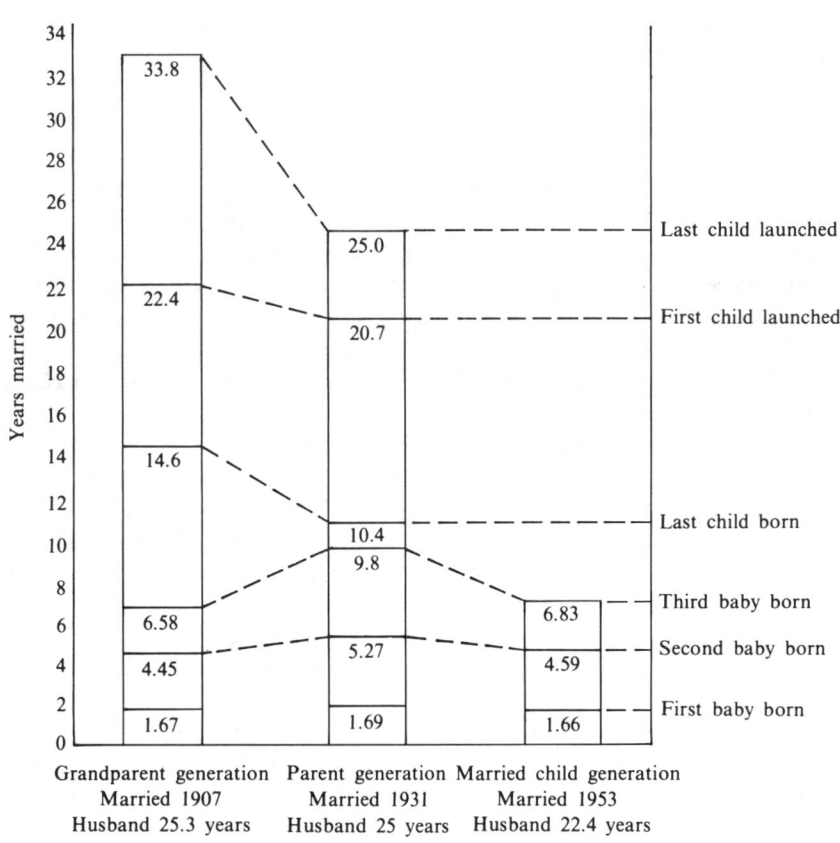

Source: From *Family Development in Three Generations* by R. Hill, N. Foote, J. Aldous, R. Carlson, and R. Macdonald. Copyright 1970 by Schenkman Publishing Company. Used by permission.

The American family profile has been changing. In 1960, the percentage of children remained about the same as in 1900, but there were fewer family members between twenty and thirty-five years and more older people. It does not require much imagination to see the deep consequences of different family compositions on family life. Some of these points will be discussed further in Chapter 8.

If we could develop a good theory of family development, it would be most useful to be able to include significant changes in role complexes and styles of interacting, particularly in later life. Most family development theorists agree that *ontogenetic development* of offspring (or simply, the development of individuals) provides order for the interactional processes and role alignments of all members of the family system. Some current thinking has even gone beyond this point to consider the reciprocal influence of several generations in the family upon each other, each generation in turn being affected by its own position in the human life course. For instance, there may be different triggering events or crises at different times of life that enter into the equation. The empty nest, retirement from jobs, or widowhood are undoubtedly important marking-off points, and there may be other significant transitions as well. Until we have more longitudinal theory and research on a variety of families, we can only speculate.

Choice of Unit

One of the major issues in studying families over time is the *choice of unit*. Should we focus on individuals and look at how they interact with other family members? This is the basis of the diagram in Table 2.2. When we focus on individuals, a family might be considered to end when the index person leaves it, either by moving out (e.g., to marry and found a new family), by death, or by divorce.

Individual. Even when our focus is so restricted, Table 2.2, which charts some of the emergent and shifting *individual* roles over life, gives a hint of the complexity of family relationships. The dotted lines symbolize the flexibility of timing of various life events; the question marks indicate that many of the roles are not necessarily a part of everyone's life. It is obvious from looking at this diagram that the middle part of life is a time when the number and kinds of relationships are most diverse and numerous, perhaps most pressing. On the one end are parents or parents-in-law, whose need for help is growing. On the other end are maturing children, starting their own adult lives with new kinds of family connections and needing parental support of various kinds. And in the middle are continuing spousal and other intragenerational relationships that may be even increasing in centrality. We know very little about how being caught in this kind of squeeze can affect the individual man and woman in midlife, but we do know that many

Table 2.2. Changing Family Roles over Life

Chronological Age	0	10	20	30	40	50	60	70	80	90
Filial		Dependent child	Transition to adult status	Adult/adult relations with parents			Dependent parents?			
Marital?			Spouse/ spouse	Spouse/parent to spouse/parent			Spouse/spouse		Widowhood?	
Parental?				Child-rearing: preschool	School age	Ado-les-cent	Empty-ing nest	Adult/adult relations with children	Dependent on children?	
Grandparental?						Grandparent?			Great-grandparent?	

clinicians and researchers have pointed to these middle years (if we remain vague about specific chronological ages) as times of crisis.

Couple.   Another way to study family development is to use the *couple* as a unit. The family in this case would start with the wedding (or, perhaps, with the first "date") and would end when one member left, whether by divorce or death. Much of traditional family theory and research uses this unit alone or in undifferentiated conjunction with the unit of the individual. Such an approach can be treacherous if it assumes unity among the two members of the couple, so that either member can speak for the couple itself. This problem will be noted later. In studying families in later life, the couple unit has considerable value, since the dividing point between early and later life is often set at the *launching period,* that is, when the couple is alone together again. As we note repeatedly in this book, this period has lengthened significantly in recent years. Research on the families of later life tends to use the couple unit from the launching stage to widowhood (or divorce) and then to revert to the individual as a unit. The implications of such shifts are not always specified.

Family System.   A third way is to view the family as a *system,* to some extent independent of any of the individuals or couples within it. In this case, the family would continue to exist beyond the individual lives of any of the persons who comprise it at any given point in time. It would be the system itself—the organization and patterning of interrelationships—whose stability or change we would study. Duvall (1971), in speaking of the *generation spiral,* says, "As older family members disappear in death, their family life cycles fade away, but their emotional, intellectual, cultural, biological, material, and personal legacies continue on through the generation spiral of which they have been a part in their own family life cycle" (p. 125). Following the heuristic thesis that Hess and Handel (1959) proposed of "family themes," and some implications of this thesis for generational research drawn by Troll and Bengtson (1978), this unit may be used more in the future.

There are many ways families may develop. Some develop with an original couple intact and in unbroken connection with both sets of relatives, their own offspring, and the relatives they produce. Other couples split, causing a wide variety of changes in the total family organization, which have so far gone virtually unstudied. What most family writers call the *family life cycle* represents only the time progression of the first, more common, and more normative group in which a couple marries, has children, and stays together until one spouse dies, presumably in old age. Even within this normative mode, constructs of the family life cycle vary from simple (Glick and Parke, 1965; Duvall, 1971; Rollins and Feldman, 1970) to complex (Hill and Rodgers, 1964). An example of a relatively simple scheme, adapted from Rollins and Feldman (1970), is shown in Table 2.3.

Communality in Family Relations Versus Uniqueness and Variety

The use of the plural *families* in the title of this book was deliberate. We want to stress our conviction that families differ widely on most parameters. Many discussions of American family life imply a universality to family processes and family development that can be dangerously misleading. Although abstracting the more general characteristics of American families is a useful and necessary step both in research and in social policy making (see Chapter 8), this focus has had the effect of emphasizing communalities over variety. Relatively few studies show *differences:* by age, sex, social class, financial status, foreign birth, rural or urban residence, ethnic origin, and so on. We must remember that for every generalization we make, there are wide group and individual differences. This is particularly true in policy and practice. Programs for Spanish-American families, for example, should be based upon as much information about Spanish-speaking families as can be obtained, and should not assume that what is true about black families is equally true about families of Spanish origin,

Table 2.3. A Simple Model of the Family Life Cycle

Beginning families (couples married 0 to 10 years without children)
Early childbearing (oldest child under 3)
Families with preschool children (oldest child over 5 and under 13)
Families with teenagers (oldest child over 12 and living at home)
Families as launching centers (oldest child gone to youngest's leaving home)
Families of middle years (empty nest to retirement)
Families in retirement (one spouse retired to onset of disability)
Families in old age (one spouse disabled to death of one spouse)

even if they have the same educational and income status and live side by side in the inner city. Future research, we hope, will produce systematic group comparisons that will enlarge our understanding of differences, similarities, and universalities alike.

Within the family, historical or generational differences may override class, financial, or ethnic differences. What is true of immigrant grandparents at the beginning of this century may not be true of their college-educated grandchildren today, and there is no reason to assume it will be true of generations yet to come. For example, people born in the 1930s generally have fewer siblings than those born in the 1950s.

If American family structure is anything, it is diverse. Around 5 percent of older people today have no spouse, no children, and no brothers and sisters. A majority of older people, though, have at least two children, as well as grandchildren, and at least 40 percent of the older population have great-grandchildren. This does not count brothers and sisters. While a few older persons have no kin at all, others are part of a complex kinship network.

As mentioned earlier, the intent of this book is to focus not only on the more common and normative family relationships, but also to show that many of today's individuals and families experience variant kinds of family patterns in both the first and second halves of their lives.

Conflict, Negotiation, and Cooperation

The dynamic and changing nature of family relationships over time has been mentioned already in several contexts. Where people are close, conflict may be inevitable at some times, harmony at others. The whole issue of *conflict* and its negotiation is vital to the study of family relationships, not only in early life, but in later life as well. One of the key questions needing further research is whether or not emotions cool off over time or with aging. If emotions do subside with time, we would expect less conflict, less need for negotiation, and more cooperation in later marriage and later family relationships. Another question concerns the handling of conflict. Who gives in to whom? Under what conditions do conflicts lead to complete breaks in family contacts: divorce, alienation, geographic separation without contact? What alliances are formed? There is unfortunately as yet little information we can draw on to examine this issue.

Disengagement

An early and continuing theme underlying gerontological theory and research over the past twenty years is the progressive *disengagement* of aging individuals from involvement in life's roles. In part, this is the consequence of "natural" losses, such as deaths of parents, spouse, and friends, or retirement from the job world. In part, disengagement is presumed to be a withdrawal of individuals upon realization of their mortality and the finiteness of their lives—a preparation for death, the final disengagement. Thus, society's exclusion of older people would coincide with older people's own withdrawal. The theory, as first stated by Cumming and Henry (1961), included a hypothetical "bonus" of higher morale for those individuals who disengaged the most. In subsequent years, surveys generally confirmed the findings of the University of Chicago's Kansas City studies on aging that there is a progressive withdrawal from social roles by older people, or at least by some older people (Youmans, 1963; Rosow, 1967). Not all people reach total uninvolvement, however, and some people don't seem to withdraw at all (Havighurst et al., 1969; Maddox, 1968; Cottrell and Atchley, 1969; Atchley, 1971; Streib and Schneider, 1971). The issue of morale, in particular, does not seem to be simple or clear-cut. Disengaging is not automatically related to higher morale. Since Cumming and Henry (1961), in their initial statement of the theory, had assumed that the disengagement process was "natural" in serving to prepare for eventual death, they had predicted that people who disengaged most would be most content and peaceful. Later research did not find any connection between amount of disengagement and either awareness of death or peacefulness of living. For one thing, morale is higher for people who disengage less. For another, it is related more to previous lifestyles than to age (Lowenthal, 1977; Neugarten, 1968). So far as the family is concerned, a third finding indicates that people may disengage from most of their societal roles, but they rarely disengage from those family roles which remain to them. As Neugarten (1968) has noted, they disengage *into,* not *from* their families. Unfortunately, aside from such generalizations and some survey data on family interactions of older people, there has been relatively little substantive research on the many corollary issues involved. We need to know a lot more about the quality of couple and parent/child relationships in later life, for example. Is disengagement into the family essentially passive, is it a negative step of retreat, or is it an active seeking of enduring values? Is it a meaningless repetition of old behaviors or a "silent intimacy"? We look forward to more questions and more answers in this area.

The disengagement theory has been reviewed by a number of gerontologists (see Atchley, 1977, pp. 209–213; Hochschild, 1975). What concerns us here is that both proponents and critics of the theory agree that the family remains an important focus of the aging individual's social interactions, providing major social supports for older members (even though the quality of interactions, as suggested by Cumming and Henry [1961], probably does change). At any rate, viewing the later stages of the family cycle as a disengagement process is not consistent with current research findings.

Perspectives

In 1960, Hill and Hansen identified and discussed five conceptual approaches used to study the family: *interactional, structural-functional, developmental, institutional, and situational*. By 1971, only three of these approaches were being utilized in most family research and theory: interactional, structural-functional, and developmental. Broderick (1971) found that the general orientation and concepts of the situational framework had been subsumed into the interactional framework by Sheldon Stryker (1964). Furthermore, the institutional approach was subsumed into the structural-functional conceptual framework. More recently, Hays (1977) found a great mixture in the training, teaching, research, and counseling of family sociologists, with the "big three" remaining the preeminent approaches in family theory: structural-functional, symbolic interactional, and developmental (Hays, 1977).

Developmental Perspective

A family developmental model includes concepts of family *role positions* (husband, wife), *role sequences* (changes in roles over time), *role clusters* (sets of roles played by each family member at any given time), and *role complexes* (sets of role clusters played concurrently by two or more incumbents of positions in an interlocking system). Unfortunately, this model, which incorporates ideas of Hill and Rodgers

(1964), Duvall (1971) and Farber (1966), is more readily adapted to a nuclear family model with implied firm boundaries than to any modified extended family with permeable boundaries among at least lineal units. It can only be applied to husband/wife interactions of later-life families, and ignores all continuing parent/child, grandparental, or sibling role complexes, though each of these other role complexes could be treated as nuclear units that can be linked together (Back, 1965). It may be possible to modify the nuclear conception of older families by including more positions (e.g., grandparents) than are included within the household limits or by having an overlapping system of role complexes. At any rate, whatever theories may be built in the future, they will have to accommodate connections with what have been considered extended kin, and be as applicable to constricting processes in family dynamics as to expanding ones.

As we mentioned earlier, different kinds of developmental schemes or models are possible. The Rollins and Feldman model presented (Table 2.3) is representative in basing the early stages upon the ontogenetic development of the children being reared and basing the three final stages upon the couple alone again (see Chapter 3). It is useful for studying the isolated nuclear family more than a modified extended family. Duvall's model in Table 2.4 differs from the Rollins and Feldman model primarily in focusing upon *developmental tasks* to be accomplished at each putative stage rather than the number of role positions present. However, it also bases earlier stages upon early childrearing and the ontogenetic progression of young children, and later stages upon the couple alone again. From one point of view, however, the Duvall model is adaptable to study of the family life cycle; it follows a marital couple through time, once it has been formed—and provided it is not dissolved.

A distinction between family development and individual development rests in the *interactional* nature of families. The life course of an individual family member may parallel changes in the family of which he or she is a part, but these processes are not identical. Development in families occurs only if there is change in the relationship or interactional character of their members: for example, if aging parents change *together with* their children. Blenkner (1965) so aptly refers to the necessity for adult children to achieve *filial maturity* if they are going to be able to accept their parents' aging and fulfill the demands for help and support this entails. But adult children cannot achieve filial maturity if their aging parents are not also achieving reciprocal parental maturity. In fact, the concept of development as an interactional and reciprocal process *at any age* may come to be one of the most significant contributions of family developmental theory that covers the whole of life.

The concept of *generations* has been mentioned in two contexts in this chapter: sources of variation among families and Duvall's idea of the generational spiral. Recently, Troll and Bengtson (1978, p. 2) noted the importance of intergenerational processes: "The generation process within the family simultaneously exerts an influence upon, and is influenced by, the generational process in an individual's development throughout the course of life and by the succession of age cohorts in the larger society." Mannheim (1952, p. 7) has also noted: "Family members are continuously changing; over time the grandparents die and are replaced by their descendents, who thereby assume different kinds of relationships with other family members. The members themselves change, partly in response to interaction with each other, partly as a consequence of maturational and social change. And historical processes can alter the character of any or all coexistent generations." Yet in spite of the fact that intergenerational processes are central to theory regarding both individual development and societal change, Troll and Bengtson (1978) pointed out that incorporation of generational concepts into family research is minimal. It is our belief that a more meaningful model of development in families will include such generational processes, as well as some of the others noted.

Problems

Because we are focusing in this book on an expanded interpretation of the concept of *family,* incorporating new views and new syntheses of issues relating to families, we face problems that most traditional family textbooks do not. Some of these problems include norms, intervening variables, and methodology.

Norms

From earliest childhood, we learn the "right" way for families to be: the right way to be a child, the right way to be a parent, a wife, a husband, a grandparent, a brother, a sister. We learn that it is important to free ourselves from our parents when we finish adolescence, just as it is important for parents of late adolescents to let go of their children. While rules like these can be helpful in providing guidelines, too often they can hamper us in finding new appropriate ways to live in a rapidly changing society. Changing beliefs about sexuality, proper male and female characteristics, childbearing and childrearing, dependence and independence, or the role of jobs in life all run counter to many traditional family norms.

Early theories of life-span human development found expedient the use of the idea of stages, expressed in terms of *developmental tasks*. Such a scheme is presented by Elizabeth Duvall (1977) in the fifth edition of her book on family development, reproduced on pages 26–31 as Table 2.4. If we look at some of the tasks she lists, particularly from late childhood on, we see the *normative* ("ought to") nature of many of them. Thus, in late childhood, we are supposed to free ourselves from "primary identification with adults" and to turn to peers. In early adolescence, we should learn our role in heterosexual relationships. In late adolescence, we should "build" a strong mutual affectional bond with a (possible) marriage partner. In maturity, we should assist our children to become independent and autonomous beings, meet "wisely the new needs for affection" of our aging parents, become good parents and grandparents, and make good sexual adjustment in marriage. In aging, we should accept "graciously and comfortably the help needed from others as powers fail and dependence becomes necessary." We should also face loss of our spouse and find some satisfactory sources of affection previously received from him or her. We should learn new affectional roles with our own children, now mature adults, and establish ongoing, satisfying patterns of affection with grandchildren and other members of the extended family, as well as finding and preserving mutually satisfying friendships outside the family circle.

Like all restrictive prescriptions for behavior, these rules ignore many of today's changing conditions. What is more, they also assume a situation that has existed for only a few members of our society at any time. The use of such terms as *appropriate, wholesome, wise, good,* and *adjustment,* among others, signals the normative nature of these tasks. They are *musts*. They allow no leeway or modifications, and little variation. They are very hard to live up to, or to live by, particularly for people who are following a different path in life.

One of the effects of such stereotypes is to distort the way we see ourselves as well as the way we see others. The stories in Chapter 1 of people who didn't see themselves as belonging to families or who didn't see that their relations with their parents were family relationships are examples of this attitude. Another is described by Bengtson and Kuypers (1971) as the *generational stake*. In this study, when youths and their parents were asked about their values and attitudes, they showed substantial agreement. Yet the youths tended to exaggerate the difference between themselves and their parents, and their parents tended to exaggerate the similarities. According to Bengtson and Kuypers, the young people were trying hard to differentiate themselves from their parents while their parents wanted to believe that their values were being transmitted, that they had done a good job of socializing their children. While this discrepancy is partly due to the effects of being at different points of the life course, it also demonstrates the distorting effect of stereotypes.

Another effect of such stereotypes is that we use them to judge our worth as children or parents—or in other family roles. For example, Troll and Turner (1976) call the condition of many middle-aged women the *Cassandra complex*. Cassandra, you may recall, was the Trojan princess who always predicted doom (and, for the Trojans, she was right). Middle-aged women of today sense the possibility of doom from several simultaneous sets of family norms. They must be concerned for their young-adult children. Are they (the children) doing the proper things for their age—getting married and having children and getting started on jobs and careers? If they are not, their mothers know that they have failed to raise proper children. At the same time, our modern Cassandras are concerned about their husbands' job success and health. They believe that both these areas reflect on the good jobs they—the wives—have done. They are also concerned about their filial responsibilities to their aging parents and parents-in-law. All the while, most of these women are themselves back in the labor market trying to catch up on postponed personal ambitions and wishes of earlier years, according to the simultaneously prevailing norms for self-realization. Some of them are finding themselves displaced homemakers, too easily discarded by their husbands, from whom they had been led to believe they would always receive loyalty and support—not only emotional but financial.

On the other hand, middle-aged men can be similarly trapped by stereotypes about family roles and relationships. Many find that the overemphasis on the provider role in our culture has isolated them from their wives and their children. To succeed as a husband and father meant first and foremost to provide the family income and this, in turn, meant putting job before family. While this at first could be considered a temporary sacrifice, eventually it became clear that "temporary" meant "until the kids are grown." Many men resent it when their

Table 2.4. Developmental Tasks in Ten Categories of Behavior of

	Infancy (birth to 1 or 2)	Early childhood (2–3 to 5–6–7)	Late childhood (5–6–7 to pubescence)
I Achieving an appropriate dependence-independence pattern	1. Establishing oneself as a very dependent being 2. Beginning the establishment of self-awareness	1. Adjusting to less private attention; becoming independent physically (while remaining strongly dependent emotionally)	1. Freeing oneself from primary identification with adults
II Achieving an appropriate giving-receiving pattern of affection	1. Developing a feeling for affection	1. Developing the ability to give affection 2. Learning to share affection	1. Learning to give as much love as one receives; forming friendships with peers
III Relating to changing social groups	1. Becoming aware of the alive as against the inanimate, and the familiar as against the unfamiliar 2. Developing rudimentary social interaction	1. Beginning to develop the ability to interact with age-mates 2. Adjusting in the family to expectations it has for the child as a member of the social unit	1. Clarifying the adult world as over against the child's world 2. Establishing peer groupness and learning to belong

Early adolescence (pubescence to puberty)	*Late adolescence (puberty to early maturity)*	*Maturity (early to late active adulthood)*	*Aging (beyond full powers of adulthood through senility)*
1. Establishing one's independence from adults in all areas of behavior	1. Establishing oneself as an independent individual in an adult manner	1. Learning to be interdependent— now leaning, now succoring others, as need arises 2. Assisting one's children to become gradually independent and autonomous beings	1. Accepting graciously and comfortably the help needed from others as powers fail and dependence becomes necessary
1. Accepting oneself as a worthwhile person really worthy of love	1. Building a strong mutual affectional bond with a (possible) marriage partner	1. Building and maintaining a strong and mutually satisfying marriage relationship 2. Establishing wholesome affectional bonds with one's children and grandchildren 3. Meeting wisely the new needs for affection of one's own aging parents 4. Cultivating meaningfully warm friendships with members of one's own generation	1. Facing loss of one's spouse, finding some satisfactory sources of affection previously received from mate 2. Learning new affectional roles with own children, now mature adults 3. Establishing ongoing, satisfying affectional patterns with grandchildren and other members of the extended family 4. Finding and preserving mutually satisfying friendships outside the family circle
1. Behaving according to a shifting peer code	1. Adopting an adult-patterned set of social values by learning a new peer code	1. Keeping in reasonable balance activities in the various social service, political, and community groups and causes that make demands on adults 2. Establishing and maintaining mutually satisfactory relationships with the in-law families of spouse and married children	1. Choosing and maintaining ongoing social activities and functions appropriate to health, energy, and interests

Table 2.4. (Cont'd.)

	Infancy (birth to 1 or 2)	Early childhood (2–3 to 5–6–7)	Late childhood (5–6–7 to pubescence)
IV Developing a conscience	1. Beginning to adjust to the expectations of others	1. Developing the ability to take directions and to be obedient in the presence of authority 2. Developing the ability to be obedient in the absence of authority where conscience substitutes for authority	1. Learning more rules and developing true morality
V Learning one's psycho-socio-biological sex role		1. Learning to identify with male adult and female adult roles	1. Beginning to identify with one's social contemporaries of the same sex
VI Accepting and adjusting to a changing body	1. Adjusting to adult feeding demands 2. Adjusting to adult cleanliness demands 3. Adjusting to adult attitudes toward genital manipulation	1. Adjusting to expectations resulting from one's improving muscular abilities 2. Developing sex modesty	

Early adolescence (pubescence to puberty)	Late adolescence (puberty to early maturity)	Maturity (early to late active adulthood)	Aging (beyond full powers of adulthood through senility)
	1. Learning to verbalize contradictions in moral codes, as well as discrepancies between principle and practice, and resolving these problems in a responsible manner	1. Coming to terms with the violations of moral codes in the larger as well as in the more intimate social scene, and developing some constructive philosophy and method of operation 2. Helping children to adjust to the expectations of others and to conform to the moral demands of the culture	1. Maintaining a sense of moral integrity in the face of disappointments and disillusionments in life's hopes and dreams
1. Strong identification with one's own sex mates 2. Learning one's role in heterosexual relationships	1. Exploring possibilities for a future mate and acquiring "desirability" 2. Choosing an occupation 3. Preparing to accept one's future role in manhood or womanhood as a responsible citizen of the larger community	1. Learning to be a competent husband or wife, and building a good marriage 2. Carrying a socially adequate role as citizen and worker in the community 3. Becoming a good parent and grandparent as children arrive and develop	1. Learning to live on a retirement income 2. Being a good companion to an aging spouse 3. Meeting bereavement of spouse adequately
1. Reorganizing one's thoughts and feelings about oneself in the face of significant bodily changes and their concomitants 2. Accepting the reality of one's appearance	1. Learning appropriate outlets for sexual drives	1. Making a good sex adjustment within marriage 2. Establishing healthful routines of eating, resting, working, playing within the pressures of the adult world	1. Making a good adjustment to failing powers as aging diminishes strengths and abilities

Table 2.4. (Cont'd.)

	Infancy (birth to 1 or 2)	Early childhood (2–3 to 5–6–7)	Late childhood (5–6–7 to pubescence)
VII Managing a changing body and learning new motor patterns	1. Developing physiological equilibrium 2. Developing eye-hand coordination 3. Establishing satisfactory rhythms of rest and activity	1. Developing large muscle control 2. Learning to coordinate large muscles and small muscles	1. Refining and elaborating skill in the use of small muscles
VIII Learning to understand and control the physical world	1. Exploring the physical world	1. Meeting adult expectations for restrictive exploration and manipulation of an expanding environment	1. Learning more realistic ways of studying and controlling the physical world
IX Developing an appropriate symbol system and conceptual abilities	1. Developing preverbal communication 2. Developing verbal communication 3. Rudimentary concept formation	1. Improving one's use of the symbol system 2. Enormous elaboration of the concept pattern	1. Learning to use language actually to exchange ideas or to influence one's hearers 2. Beginning understanding of real causal relations 3. Making finer conceptual distinctions and thinking reflectively
X Relating oneself to the cosmos		1. Developing a genuine, though uncritical, notion about one's place in the cosmos	1. Developing a scientific approach

Source: From *Family Development* by Evelyn M. Duvall, Copyright © 1977. Reprinted by permission of the publisher, J. B. Lippincott Company.

Early adolescence (pubescence to puberty)	Late adolescence (puberty to early maturity)	Maturity (early to late active adulthood)	Aging (beyond full powers of adulthood through senility)
1. Controlling and using a "new" body		1. Learning the new motor skills involved in housekeeping, gardening, sports, and other activities expected of adults in the community	1. Adapting interests and activities to reserves of vitality and energy of the aging body
		1. Gaining intelligent understanding of new horizons of medicine and science sufficient for personal well-being and social competence	1. Mastering new awareness and methods of dealing with physical surroundings as an individual with occasional or permanent disabilities
1. Using language to express and to clarify concepts 2. Moving from the concrete to the abstract and applying general principles to the particular	1. Achieving the level of reasoning of which one is capable	1. Mastering technical symbol systems involved in income tax, social security, complex financial dealings, and other contexts familiar to Western man	1. Keeping mentally alert and effective as long as is possible through the later years
	1. Formulating a workable belief and value system	1. Formulating and implementing a rational philosophy of life on the basis of adult experience 2. Cultivating a satisfactory religious climate in the home as the spiritual soil for development of family members	1. Preparing for eventual and inevitable cessation of life by building a set of beliefs that one can live and die with in peace

wives and children show alienation and hostility, instead of under-standing and support, at what they, the husbands and fathers, see as a necessary overinvolvement with their jobs. Many husbands and fathers are genuinely puzzled at having done what they were "sup-posed to," only to see their wives leave, taking their children with them. Such men sometimes end up feeling alone, supporting two households, and trying to meet filial obligations to older parents with-out much preparation for the task.

These problems may be more typical of the white middle class, but other classes also suffer from the gaps between cultural norms and the achievable realities. Much of the current variety of family stan-dards and lifestyles can be viewed as the process through which societies change their ideas about what ought to be and the resulting change in stereotypes. Many norms today are transitional. We have moved away from old norms of what constitutes acceptable family behavior but have not yet been able to find or accept new ones. In a way we are all Cassandras now, men and women, young, old, and middle aged.

Intervening Variables

All aspects of family interaction are affected by *intervening variables* generated by individuals on one hand and society at large on the other. These variables include finances, health, social status, and longevity.

Finances. Socioeconomic status, social class, level of living, and *income decline* all affect most parameters of family life. When we deal with families in later life, in particular, we must consider not only the current financial state, but also whether the current state is the same or different from earlier states and whether the financial status of older generations is relatively lower than that of later generations in the same family. The fact that most people over age sixty-five in our coun-try are below what is considered the poverty level is important in many ways because it determines how well they can dress, eat, move around, get good medical attention, and remain physically and financially inde-pendent. The fact that many of them have experienced financial depri-vation as a result of retirement provides other important sets of conse-quences, including such psychological factors as how they respect themselves and how many earlier habits they have to change. The fact that many are worse off than their children and grandchildren provides a third set of consequences, including their value to their children and grandchildren as respected people toward whom to turn for advice and attention. Family elders with maintained—or increased—power and wealth are likely to be regarded quite differently from family elders about whose daily economic requirements their descendants must be concerned. Even when physically enfeebled, the more financially advantaged set of elders have very different family positions than the less advantaged.

Health.   *Health* is a critical variable in almost all aspects of the life of older people. Studies of retirement show that health is antecedent to activity and thus to life satisfaction (Atchley, 1977). It influences isolation, dependency, and mood. As in economics, not only are *absolute* levels of health important, but also *relative* health. This seems to be particularly true for husband/wife relations. The fact that most older men have married younger women and that women's life expectancy is longer underlies much of the power differential and quality of life of both spouses. If a relatively younger and stronger woman must nurse an older and weaker husband—in many cases, for a year or more before he dies—she gains a certain kind of ascendency over him, but she may also become a virtual slave, confined to her home.

Longevity.   Historical changes in life expectancy and mortal ity, together with sex differences in these indices, have profound effects upon family relationships. Some of the consequences are the presence of more older grandparents and great-grandparents, and the anticipation of many more years of post-childrearing life together for husbands and wives. In some cases, the prospects of a long life together may seem so forbidding that they can lead to increases in divorce at all ages. Changes in the age profile of families from two broad generations to four or five narrow generations can affect the way people feel toward each other and the decisions they make about their own lives. These points will be discussed in later chapters.

Methodological Problems

Some of the problems encountered by people who study families are not the result of substantive problems such as cultural stereotypes or intervening variables such as level of living or health, but instead come from within the *knowledge system* we use to study families. The knowledge-generating system presents us with problems arising from conceptual confusion, research methodology, and academic norms and rewards. None of these problems is devastating, but readers of this book need to be aware of the difficulties that confronted those whose research is summarized here.

Conceptual Confusion. *Conceptual confusion* is unavoidable so long as we deal with languages in which a single word can have numerous meanings. In social sciences it is important to keep in mind that most of our concepts do not refer to concrete, observable objects in our environment, such as a stone or a table, but to symbols of a more general kind. For example, the concept *social role* does not refer to any one person or kind of person but is derived from the interaction among occupants of positions. It does not even tell us what those interactions might be. Even the more specific concept *wife role* suggests only a few general characteristics; the other characteristics of that role must be discovered through further study and can easily vary depending on the influence of still other characteristics such as age, marital duration, social class, and ethnicity.

When we discuss the general relationship between two abstract concepts such as social class and the parent/child relation, we are not referring to anything *real*. We are making a general statement derived from information about a host of actual parent/child relationships. Such statements necessarily leave out the range of variability, and simplifications can lead to inappropriate and dangerous applications. Every generalization in social science has exceptions, sometimes important ones, and this is why trying to make inferences from general social science theory to specific cases is not a mechanical task but instead a subtle art that requires both in-depth knowledge and experience as well as sensitivity to the uniqueness of a particular situation.

Most analysis in social science assumes cause and effect. To avoid conceptual confusion on this score, it is important to set up research to examine several possible causes simultaneously. For example, marital satisfaction can presumably be influenced by numerous factors: marital duration, presence of children in the home, financial well-being, health, and so forth. It is not enough to look simply at the correlation between marital satisfaction and marital duration. We want to put marital duration's effect in a context, to evaluate the causal power of marital duration compared to other causes of marital satisfaction.

Another conceptual difficulty stems from confusing terminology. This type of confusion can result from a lack of appropriate terminology or from too many terms for the same thing. Kinship terminology is especially troublesome. On one hand, there is no accepted term for the family comprised of an adult couple, their parents, and their children. *Three-generation family, immediate family,* and *lineal family* have been used to describe this type of family, but all these expressions currently suffer from a certain amount of ambiguity. On the other hand, using three different expressions to describe the same entity also leads to confusion.

Research Methodology. Research methodology can also create difficulties. Often the unit of interest is not the unit sampled. For example, studies of married couples very often obtain information from samples made up of only one member of the couple. Studies of multigenerational relations seldom get information from all family members involved because it is very costly and time consuming. Too often, one person's version of a complex network of family relations is taken as representative.

Bridging the gap between abstract concepts and concrete indicators (or measures) of those concepts is often difficult. For example, the expression *marital satisfaction* is a general, sensitizing concept. Not only do conceptual definitions of marital satisfaction vary considerably, so do the questions or observations used to measure it. Readers have a tendency to forget that research deals with *indicators* of concepts, not the concepts directly. They tend to think that a morale measure for a person is morale for that person. Unfortunately, operational indicators vary greatly in how closely they correspond to the concept. For example, subjective measures of health have been found to approximate physicians' reports quite closely. But measures of self-esteem may not really tell us how people feel about themselves. Conflicting research results often can be traced to variations in indicators used. This problem is compounded by the fact that scores of indicators exist for concepts such as social class, intelligence, morale, self-esteem, or marital satisfaction.

Data collection is never easy, but it is especially difficult in the area of family relations. Contrary to popular belief, ours is a very family-oriented society. As a result, people are often reluctant to discuss honestly problems that may exist in marital relations or intergenerational relations. Likewise, researchers often put people on the spot by asking them to talk about feelings they have never even thought about before. Respondents will give an answer, but answers "off the top of the head" are not always accurate.

A problem permeating all life-span research is that of errors from generalizing trends on the basis of cross-sectional data. When people of different ages or of different durations of marriage are compared at one point in time, we cannot assume that the younger or shorter-lasting relationships will be like the longer-lasting ones after the appropriate number of years. Younger people have grown up under different conditions from older ones and thus are likely to be different from the older generation at all points of their life. People who were married and became parents in the 1920s did so under markedly different circumstances from those who married and became parents in the 1930s during the Depression, in the 1940s during World War II, in the 1960s during the influence of the youth movement, or in the 1970s during the women's movement. Longitudinally collected data provide some correction for this kind of error. These are obtained by restudying the same people at intervals over the years, so "true" age changes, as opposed to age differences, can be assessed. Even longitudinal data are subject to error, however, because they do not take account of period changes—historical events and circumstances that affect all who live at a particular time, regardless of their age. Besides, they have their own sources of error, including survivor bias. Schaie (1967) proposes cross-sequential or time-sequential research to assess more generalized developmental changes. Such procedures would combine both cross-sectional data (several different age or duration groups measured at the same point in time) with longitudinal or cohort data. Most family data at the present time are cross-sectional. Where we are discussing longitudinal data (there are as yet no cross-sequential or time-sequential data on families), we will so indicate.

Numerous other methodological problems could be discussed, but our purpose here is not to write a definitive methodological treatise. We only want to convey the notion that research is a process beset with problems, some more difficult than others, carried out by human beings—with all the fallibility that implies. The product of research is more often a fuzzy picture with vague but generally recognizable features rather than a crisp portrait in which everything is in focus and elegantly arranged. Unfortunately, a good deal of retouching goes on in the process of writing research reports, and the dilemmas of the research process are seldom revealed.

Scientific Conventions and Rewards. The *conventions* and *rewards* of the system we use in order to create and accumulate knowledge also cause difficulties. Most family researchers are social scientists. Right now, the social sciences are dominated by several biases. And what's "in" at any point in time affects rewards for research work. In some current social science, as reflected in the publishing policies of major journals, acceptable research is supposed to be deduced from classical theory rather than induced from empirical observations. Beyond this, large samples are the order of the day, and graduate students are encouraged to select dissertation topics that use "available data." Furthermore, quantitative data are given preference over qualitative data. All of these current conventions limit our information about families in later life. Unfortunately, we have not been studying such families for decades and thus have not accumulated the kind of descriptive or theoretical base we could use as a springboard for more sophisticated social science research. Current investigators of families in later life are pioneers. They are often operating in uncharted territory, and the prevailing scholarly system simply is not set up to reward people who pioneer. Publications, grant funds, and recognition are all harder to get for those who lay out the basic descriptive dimensions of a new territory than for those who do deductive theory testing in established areas.

Summary

Numerous controversies exist in the study of families in later life. In our opinion, the weight of the evidence shows that older people generally are not isolated but are part of an extended family, that family studies are inconclusive on the question of whether the family ties of older adults are primarily instrumental or intimate, and that cross-sectional studies have stressed structure and stability in family relationships at the expense of the perhaps more typical process of ebb and flow. Whether change in family relationships tends to be gradual or the result of a sudden crisis remains to be resolved. Whether there is a generation gap depends on where you look. Similarities between generations can be found, but so can differences. Social change has increased the number of generations in the family but reduced the size of each generation. Whether research focuses on individuals, couples, or the family system has important implications for the uses to which it can be put. Whether research focuses on similarities among families or on uniqueness and variety also has important implications. Research on family relations needs to focus more sharply on processes such as conflict, cooperation, and negotiation to get a clearer picture of family dynamics. Disengagement, when it occurs, tends to be *into* the family rather than from it.

Perspectives that can be used to study families include developmental, structural-functional, and interactional-generational. All these perspectives have their appropriate uses.

Problems that make it difficult to study families in later life include norms and stereotypes that steer research and common sense away from realities of family life; intervening variables, such as finances, health, and longevity, that introduce variations; conceptual confusion, such as ambiguous language and faulty conceptualization of research issues; and problems of research methodology, such as measurement and sampling. While these problems represent true concerns, research goes on and much of it is well done.

Chapter Three

Older Couples*

Prevalence of Marriage in Later Life

Most adult Americans are married and live with their spouses in their own households. In fact, at some time in their adult life almost all Americans have been married (nearly 95 percent). As Table 1.1 shows, however, there is a gradual reduction with age in the proportion of older Americans who are still part of a couple. This reduction becomes noticeable after the age of fifty, particularly for women, and even more particularly for poorer and black women. After age seventy-five, while 70 percent of the men have a living wife, only 23 percent of the women have a living husband. In this chapter we discuss the relationships between husbands and wives in later life, how these are affected by economic and health circumstances and retirement, how the general index of *marital satisfaction* changes over time, what we know about household divisions of labor, sexuality, and remarriage and, finally, the effect of retirement upon marital relations.

Longer Empty Nest Period

Over the last century, the average number of years a couple lives together after their children leave home has increased greatly (Glick, 1977). Today the *empty nest* transition occurs in middle age.

*Part of this chapter is adapted from Troll and Turner, 1976.

rather than in old age. A number of factors have contributed to this lengthening post-childrearing period.

1. The average life expectancy has increased; more people are living to older ages.
2. The age of childbearing has decreased, at least until 1972; more recent census figures are ambiguous about whether a new trend toward later average age of having the first child is a temporary effect of one cohort's delay in getting married and having a child, or the beginning of a new long-term effect.
3. The number of children per family has decreased as a partial consequence of birth control practices.
4. Children are born within a few years of each other instead of being spaced throughout the fertile years of the woman.

This lengthening of the "couple alone again" period has been accompanied by a number of new patterns of relationships between husbands and wives, most of them still unstudied. Many contradictory statements have appeared in the family literature. For example, there are popular reports that marriages are more likely to break up when the children leave home, with a secondary peaking in divorce rates comparable to that of beginning marriage (so far unsupported by any demographic data). These reports are counterbalanced by other reports of the phenomenon of *second honeymoons* when husband and wife are alone again. There are statements that women are more affected or more changed in their feelings and behavior by the emptying of the nest than their husbands, but nobody has done systematic research on how fathers are affected by this situation. Furthermore, others have said that couples now have greater opportunity for sharing activities, both household chores and leisure activities, and that this leads to greater enjoyment of their marriage. There are reports that sexuality terminates for most couples at this time, counterbalanced by reports of revitalized sexuality. There are reports of heightened marital satisfaction—but these are often tied to reports of cooling down of interpersonal interactions. Unfortunately, most of our research information is still so tenuous for these later years that we must proceed cautiously in drawing anything but tentative conclusions. It would not be too far-fetched to presume that diversity of marital style in later years is even greater than in earlier years. After all, variation increases in almost every other measure with each succeeding decade of life. Thus, it is possible that many of these statements are true, each for a different segment of the population. Let us review some of the factors leading to such diversity.

Sex Differences

Sex differences in family behavior appear to be profound. For example, Bernard (1973) concluded that marriage is an institution that benefits husbands but not wives, although women are the ones for whom it is of prime social importance. Women seem to worry much more than men about their families, especially in middle age, as we noted in Chapter 2, when we referred to them as Cassandras. For one thing, they are dismayed and disadvantaged by age changes in appearance that are interpreted as decreases in attractiveness, while men of the same age even seem to gain in attractiveness (Nowak, 1975). It is not surprising, therefore, that middle-aged women are the age/sex group most critical of their husbands and most prone to reporting difficulties in getting along with them (Lowenthal et al., 1975). Although four fifths of all men and the same proportion of newlywed and older women had a positive evaluation of their spouses, only two fifths of middle-aged women did so. Interestingly, while the men of this age stressed their wives' virtues, only one third of them thought they were meeting their wives' expectations. Thurnher reports (in Lowenthal et al., 1975) that middle-aged men did not question their adequacy as providers but seemed aware—though not necessarily contrite about it or moved to change—that they were often inconsiderate and unheeding of their wives' desires for attention, companionship, or diversion. The women mentioned their husbands when they described their daily activities, but the men did not usually mention their wives. In fact, the men tended not to mention the everyday domestic interactions that the women described. Similar to the working-class and upper-middle-class fathers described by Rubin (1975), then, these lower-middle-class middle-aged men tended to be psychologically absent from their homes even when physically present.

Many of the older women in the Lowenthal San Francisco study felt that their husbands were overdependent; among the newlyweds, it was the husbands who were more likely to express such feelings about their wives. Where the men tended to describe their dependent feelings as *tender,* the women described them as *clinging.* Although in their *Thematic Apperception Test* (*TAT*) responses, both sexes at this stage of the family life cycle yearned for warmth and intimacy in the marital relationship, women seemed less hopeful of its promise, expecting at best a relationship that provided support and staved off loneliness.

Several alternative explanations have been offered for these sex differences in marital satisfaction, particularly in middle life. Some sociologists feel that sexual politics is a reason (Bernard, 1973; Hochschild, 1973). In this view, husbands feel more satisfied with marriage because they have more power than their wives; they perceive the marriage as their choice and in their control to change if they don't like it. Another explanation offered is that a man's happiness is less dependent on his marriage than a woman's because a man can get psychic rewards from both his job and his family, whereas traditionally a woman gets psychic rewards only from her family. It is true that many women now work outside the home, but they are still underrepresented in high-status occupations, and thus, according to this view they are less likely than their husbands to derive satisfaction from their jobs. Research indicates, however, that employed women are no less likely than employed men to get satisfaction from their jobs (Cottrell and Atchley, 1969; Atchley and Corbett, 1977).

The life-span developmental literature provides evidence for consistency in coping abilities throughout life. The way women adjust to the empty nest transition, for example, will signal their adjustment to later critical events. Those women (and men) who have trouble with the events of middle age tend to be those who had trouble with transitions at earlier times of life—puberty, sex, childbearing, and so on—and who will have most trouble with later transitions, such as retirement, widowhood, and disabilities (Neugarten, 1968; Lowenthal, 1977; Maas and Kuypers, 1974).

Sex differences in marital satisfaction in later life are not found consistently. Burr (1970), Laws (1971), Lurie (1974), Rollins and Feldman (1970), and Stinnett, Collins, and Montgomery (1970) found them, but Rollins and Cannon (1974) did not. We particularly need more research on men's attitudes toward marriage and housework, as well as cross-sequential data to see whether cohort differences exist.

Social Class and Race Differences

Like sex differences, *social class differences* pervade many of our conclusions and reports. To begin with, economic and health and demographic factors are all connected with social class, and all influ-

Table 3.2. Percent Distribution of Persons by Chronic Condition and Activity Limitation Status, According to Sex and Age: United States, July 1965–June 1967

Sex and Age *Both Sexes*	*Total* *Population*	*Persons* *with No* *Chronic* *Conditions*	*Total*
All ages	100.0	50.5	49.5
Under 17 years	100.0	77.2	22.8
17–44 years	100.0	45.9	54.1
45–64 years	100.0	28.9	71.1
65 years & over	100.0	14.4	85.6
Male			
All ages	100.0	51.8	48.2
Under 17 years	100.0	75.8	24.2
17–44 years	100.0	47.4	52.6
45–64 years	100.0	30.5	69.5
65 years & over	100.0	15.6	84.4
Female			
All ages	100.0	49.3	50.7
Under 17 years	100.0	78.6	21.4
17–44 years	100.0	44.7	55.3
45–64 years	100.0	27.5	72.5
65 years & over	100.0	13.5	86.5

Source: Adapted from C. Wilder, 1971, p. 19.

more equalitarian expectations. Unfortunately, only the first of these deals with older couples. Husbands generally say their marriage is more satisfactory than do their wives. When Veroff and Feld (1970) asked people to list things about their marriages that they did not like, 45 percent of the married men said "nothing," as compared with only 25 percent of the married women. Bernard (1973) has detailed how marriage is better for husbands than for wives, as noted earlier.

There is a large body of research, mostly cross-sectional, that looks at *changes* in marital satisfaction over time. Yet trying to get either a description or an explanation for what does happen is still difficult. Cross-sectional studies that compare couples who have been married only a short time with those who have been married longer generally show a curvilinear pattern, with marital satisfaction high

ence marital interactions. Second, there are class differences in values, expectations, and interpretations. Data on black couples are not only rarer than those for white couples but frequently have not distinguished between middle-class and lower-class black couples. Thus, poor black couples are usually compared with middle-class white couples. Generally, black couples tend to be poorer, have poorer health, and live fewer years than white couples. Thus, fewer older black women live with their husbands, particularly in the South, and this racial differential is increasing rather than decreasing (Jackson, 1977). Those black women who have married are more likely to be widowed at an early age than white married women. There is also some evidence that the mother/child bond is valued more highly in black families than the husband/wife bond (Bell, 1965).

Economic Factors

The amount of money couples have to spend on their own needs and desires clearly influences the way they live and the way they feel about their life. This applies not only to the absolute amount available to them, but also to the *income pinch* they experience: the amount they have relative to the amount they need to spend. Other things being equal, young couples raising children have a greater pinch than those who do not have children or those whose children have become relatively independent economically, and post-retirement couples are usually under greater economic deprivation than before retirement. Table 3.1 shows the age distribution of poverty-level prevalence of family members by sex. It is clear that women are much more likely to live below the poverty level than men the same age, particularly when they are heads of households and thus not part of a married couple. Just considering the normative couple, however, where the husband is considered the head of the household, the percentages of households below the poverty level is almost twice as great over age sixty-five as between twenty-two and sixty-four.

There are both generational and social class differences in the timing of financial pinch. When Hill and his colleagues (1970) studied the economic situation of three generations of married couples, he found that the grandparents were relatively the most disadvantaged, both at the time they got married and throughout their married life into old age. Their children started off better and remained that way. The grandchildren couples started off the best, with the most "durable

Table 3.1.   Percent of Men and Women in Poverty, 1973

Age	Men	Women
Total age 16 or older	7.4	11.6
16–21 years	10.4	13.2
Family head	13.2	75.6
Other family member	8.3	9.3
Unrelated individual	38.1	49.6
22–64 years	5.8	9.7
Family head	4.6	33.4
Other family member	5.7	5.2
Unrelated individual	15.2	22.8
65 or older	12.4	19.0
Family head	9.5	16.8
Other family member	8.0	8.0
Unrelated individual	27.1	33.5

Source: U.S. Bureau of the Census, 1975.

goods'' and the most comfortable living arrangements, even though they experienced more financial pinch after they had a child or two. Since the third generation was still at an early stage of their family life course at the time of the study, it is hard to predict what their future economic circumstances will be like. In general, though, some generations reach old age in better economic circumstances than others.

So far as social class differences are concerned, since economic recovery of a couple begins when children can start earning money, working-class, nonmobile families tend to get back to their peak economic level earlier than middle-class couples do. In wealthier or more socially striving families, this event is postponed because of commitment to lengthier education. We must not forget, however, that the peak level we are talking about is a relative one. For poorer families, it may be much lower than the lowered level of the wealthier families.

In conclusion, we see that the average couple has a series of ups and downs in economic circumstances that should affect the strain under which they are operating. They should feel relatively expansive and in high spirits before they have children, more constricted and pinched during the time they are raising the children and educating them, freer again once the children can be more self-supporting, and more limited again after retirement if their income is limited. Couples that receive more from old age benefits than they had earned earlier in their lives may enjoy their later years together more than they had their earlier years.

Health Factors

Like economic circumstances, health can make a difference in the ease and comfort of marital relations. As men and women get older, although they tend to get fewer acute illnesses, they suffer from more chronic illnesses. This may not get to be a major factor before sixty-five, but it can become an increasingly important one after that age, as shown in Table 3.2. Since more often the husbands are older, and since men are more likely to have some limitation in activity at any given older-age decade, the effect on marriages is likely to be that of turning wives into at least part-time nurses.

Feldman (1964) found health to be a major topic of conversation between husband and wife over sixty-five years of age. He also found that wives at this time had the highest degree of power within the marital relationship. It seems likely that at least part of this enhanced power resides in physical power relative to that of their husbands (Troll and Turner, 1976). Men depend upon their wives for health care in varying degrees, from maternal nurturance (''Dear, don't forget to take your medicine'') to terminal nursing care. In her study of middle-aged urban widows, Lopata (1973) was surprised to find that as many as 46 percent of these widows had cared for their husbands at home during their final illnesses. In 40 percent of these cases, they had nursed their husbands for over a year. Not only does this kind of health problem severely curtail many kinds of marital interactions, it also reduces the wife's freedom of action.

Marital Satisfaction

Marriages are usually assessed according to two separate criteria: *happiness* and *stability*. People who have happy marriages get divorced, and people with very unhappy marriages stay together for fifty years. Happiness in marriage depends as much on each partner's expectations as on their actual relationship. Thus, the highly educated or avant-garde men and women who stress self-actualization and romantic love as a top requirement for a good marriage are not likely to tolerate the kind of relationship that would seem good to a working-class, more traditional wife who is satisfied with a portion of a paycheck and little or no companionship from her husband. Findings from three different studies—Westley and Epstein (1960), Aller (1962), and Cutter and Dyer (1965)—all show that couples with more traditional expectations for marriage say they are happier than those with

Persons with 1 Chronic Condition or More

With No Limitation of Activity	With Limitation But Not in Major Activity[a]	With Limitation in Amount or Kind of Major Activity[a]	Unable to Carry on Major Activity[a]	Total with Some Limitation
38.0	2.9	6.4	2.1	11.4
20.9	1.0	0.7	0.2	1.9
46.7	2.7	4.1	0.6	7.4
51.8	5.1	11.4	2.8	19.3
39.6	6.5	25.7	13.8	46.0
36.1	2.5	6.5	3.1	12.1
22.1	1.1	0.8	0.2	2.1
44.7	2.5	4.6	0.9	8.0
48.7	4.4	11.9	4.5	20.8
31.4	4.6	26.8	21.6	53.0
39.9	3.3	6.3	1.2	10.8
19.5	1.0	0.7	0.1	1.8
48.5	2.9	3.6	0.4	6.9
54.7	5.7	10.9	1.2	17.8
45.9	8.0	24.9	7.7	40.6

[a]Major activity refers to ability to work, keep house, or engage in school or preschool activities.

among those recently married, somewhat lower among those in the childrearing period, and higher again among those in the later stages of the family life cycle. There are reasons for caution in accepting these results as indicative of change over time, however. Even in cross-sectional studies, some *measures* of marital satisfaction do not produce a curvilinear pattern (Burr, 1970; Rollins and Feldman, 1970); nor do some *samples* of married people (Spanier, Lewis, and Coles, 1975). More sophisticated data that follow the same couples over the years are necessary in order to rule out the possibility that the higher prevalence of happy marriages in later life is simply a result of greater divorce or separation among those who are unhappily married, or that those couples who are now older were brought up to be satisfied with less.

Generations differ widely in initial commitment to marriage and in attitudes toward divorce (Spanier, Lewis, and Coles, 1975). Developmental theorists point out that the exclusive use of either cross-sectional or longitudinal designs to study developmental phenomena is inappropriate (Schaie, 1967). Cross-sectional designs may result in a *generational fallacy* by ignoring life-course differences, while longitudinal designs may produce a *life-course fallacy* by ignoring age cohort differences (Rollins and Cannon, 1974). Instead, sequential/longitudinal research designs (Nesselroade et al, 1972), which start out with groups of couples married for shorter and longer periods of time and then continue to study both groups over many years, seem most appropriate in studying the patterns of family development. So far, these kinds of studies are just being begun, and none of them is looking at the family of later life.

Survivor effects present another methodological problem. Marriages that have been ended between one round of testing or interviewing and the next have disappeared from the samples of long-term marriages. Especially from the standpoint of evaluating marital satisfaction or adjustment, cohort-related differences in divorce rates are of central importance, as are cohort-related differences in ways of responding to interviews, in conventionality, in values, and in acquiescence response sets. They may all distort the results we get.

Beyond all these problems in measuring marital satisfaction over time, there is fundamental disagreement about definitions of what is being measured and how to measure it. For example, *self-reports,* which almost all investigators have used, are extraordinarily vulnerable to such psychological distortion processes as *cognitive dissonance* (resolving the discomfort of confronting opposing facts by choosing one and denying the other). One may be likely to evaluate one's marriage as satisfactory when one perceives few other options, or when being married is the basis for all other aspects of life. Bernard (1973) points out that resignation often is reported as satisfaction, and Veroff and Feld (1970) found that those most likely to feel that their marriage was good were women with the least amount of education—and thus fewer other options.

The Childrearing Period

A theme of progressive disenchantment with marriage from the peak of the honeymoon to the nadir of middle age is reiterated in a number of investigations, both cross-sectional and longitudinal (Pineo, 1961; Blood and Wolfe, 1960; and Feldman, 1964). They all report a lowered marital satisfaction and marital adjustment after the birth of the first child which persists throughout the childrearing years. This pessimistic cast is supported by the less rigorous but creative study of Cuber and Harroff (1965), who found five types of marriages in a sample of upper-middle-class successful Americans: *conflict habituated, devitalized, passive/congenial, vital,* and *total.* The most prevalent types in middle age, alas, even in these energetic people, were the devitalized and passive/congenial.

Post-Childrearing

The post-childrearing couples Feldman interviewed reported higher satisfaction with their marriage than did couples in earlier stages, and this "upswing" seemed to be even more pronounced among the oldest couples. Similar findings are cited by Stinnett et al. (1972). Perhaps future research focusing on changes in functions and feelings in relationships over time will shed more light on this area. For example, is there a shift from *attraction* to *attachment,* or from *ardor* to *loyalty*? This will be discussed later in this chapter.

Earlier, Stinnett et al. (1970) had investigated older peoples' perceptions of how well their marriage fulfilled six emotional needs: *love, personality fulfillment, respect, communication, finding meaning in life,* and *integration of past life experiences.* The older men (age sixty or older) had significantly higher need satisfaction scores than did the older women; more of their needs were being met in the marital relationship. Significantly, the lowest need satisfaction score for men was in *respect*; for women, in *communication.*

Since the conjugal post-childrearing period can last for thirty, forty, or even more years—if the last child leaves home when the parents are in their early forties and their life expectancy is seventy or eighty years—subdivision of this period would be convenient. Thompson and Streib (1961), for instance, outline four stages of post-parental life: (1) the family of late maturity, (2) the family of preretirement, (3) the family of early retirement, and (4) the family of late retirement. This categorization may be more appropriate for the discussion of work and retirement (it is part of a volume titled *Aging and Leisure*) than for family relations. Nevertheless, it is simple and its use of the decade as a unit permits demographic comparisons. The following presentation is based on their outline, though the original demographic figures they used have been brought up to date from the most recently available U.S. Census figures (1975).

In *late maturity,* husband and wife are generally between age forty-five and fifty-four (incidentally, over 90 percent of all men and women in this age range have been married at least once by this time). The overwhelming majority at this age are couples living in their own homes (95 percent of the white men and 93 percent of the white women), and more than half of these couples still have a child under eighteen at home. In family terms, this is the *launching* stage. For the women, it is also the time of the menopause, and 54 percent of them have jobs.

In the second *preretirement* stage, the average chronological ages are fifty-five to sixty-four. The majority is still couples living in their own homes, but sex differences in survival are becoming noticeable. While 85 percent of the men are still married, only 69 percent of the women are. Now only 43 percent of the women are employed.

In the third stage, *early retirement,* the ages are sixty-five to seventy-four. During this decade, male mortality accelerates so much that it is convenient to break down the figures on marital status into five-year groupings. Over 83 percent of the men are still married, but only 49 percent of the women. Less than 10 percent of the women are employed.

In the fourth stage, *late retirement,* husband and wife—for those still together—are over seventy-five. The percent of men still married is 70; contrast this figure with that for women (23 percent). Few women (or men) are employed.

It is obvious that over the age of sixty-five, any data on marital relations are based on a sample highly biased for survival—and also include people who have been married more than once. Thus, there is no guarantee that the trends for older couples are later phases of those for younger or middle-aged couples.

Feldman (1964) finds that couples in the "launching stage," when one or more children are still at home, say they are quite satisfied with their marriages—their satisfaction is exceeded only by youthful honeymooners and the elderly. Couples say their relations tend to be calm and objective more than emotional (Cuber and Harroff's *passive/congenial* relationship). Their focus is still on their children. They spend a lot of time talking about them, and much of their interaction involves them. They still fight, but while their early fights tended to end with love-making and increased happiness, they now tend to look back without much pleasure on the course of their marriage.

Feldman's couples in the next stage, with all children out of the home and the wife under sixty-five years old, are more extreme in their behavior. They are even less satisfied with their marriage than those who still have children at home. "They place the highest values on the conjugal factors in marriage, calmness, and companionship, and a low value on the more romantic affective factors, indicating that they have come to terms with their marriage as a companionate, more sedentary venture" (pp. 141–142). On the whole, Feldman finds the two stages "similar enough in their basic dynamics even though not identical in their characteristics so that they might have been combined."

Feldman's older couples whose children have left home (wife over sixty-five) are quite different from most of the others. Their discussions are restricted in range to conventional topics such as religion and home repairs. They are preoccupied with health. They rarely have a gay time away from home, and their marital interaction is low. The wife at this time has the highest degree of power relative to her husband (perhaps as a result of health differences—see discussion in previous section). Perhaps the outstanding characteristic of this group is a general feeling of peacefulness, lack of stress, and expressed satisfaction with marriage; in the last index they approach the level of the newly married. From a comparison with a control group of childless couples married about the same length of time, Feldman concludes that for older couples "length of experience with marriage may be a more significant factor . . . than their experience with children."

Reedy (1977) found that long-married couples tended to stress loyalty and emotional security over all other important characteristics of marriage, as did Parron (1978) in a sample of "golden wedding" couples. Later in this chapter we will discuss possible changes in interaction over time.

A different cross-sectional study of four stages of adult life included two groups of middle-aged people (Lowenthal et al., 1975). The youngest child of one of these groups was a senior in high school; this was a launching stage sample. In the other group were people within three years of retirement; few still had children living at home. Lurie (1974) reported that most of the people in both these groups said that they had experienced positive changes in their marital relationship. The older group were twice as likely as the younger group to say they had experienced any change (33% versus 15%) and less likely to report negative changes in their marriages (14% versus 38%). One could hypothesize that the fewer children left in the household, the fewer parents reporting negative changes in their marriage (see Table 3.3).

Lowenthal and her associates (1975) also reported that those married people facing retirement expressed renewed interest in the personalities of their spouses. Eighty-two percent of both men and

Table 3.3.   Changes in Past Relationship with Spouses during Two Stages

Changes	Relationship (percent)	
	Empty Nest	*Preretired*
Positive	47	53
No change	15	33
Negative	38	14
Total (*N*)	(54)	(60)

Source: Adapted from E. Lurie, "Sex and Stage Differences in Perceptions of Marital and Family Relationships," *Journal of Marriage and the Family.* Copyright 1974 by the National Council on Family Relations. Used by permission.

women in this stage gave *positive* descriptions of their spouses. They felt that their *marriage* had improved since their children left home. This was particularly true for the men. People in this stage experienced greater companionship and closeness, and did not expect this to change during retirement, although they did recognize an increased *potential* for friction after retirement. The women were not looking forward to their husbands' entry into the home, and the men were not looking forward to intruding into what they perceived as their wives' domain.

While some—nearly one third—of the husbands and wives reported increasing sexual satisfaction in the period between the children's departure and retirement, many more—half of the men and one third of the women—said that their sexual relations were worse since the children had left home. This topic of sexuality is discussed more in a later section.

Maas and Kuypers (1974) have published a description of the lifestyles and personalities of 95 mothers and 47 fathers between sixty and eighty-two years of age. This longitudinal study includes 47 older couples who had originally been selected in the 1920s as parents of children whose development was to be investigated. Among these upper-middle-class California men, about 40 percent were highly involved with their wives and happy with their marriages. Another 23 percent were involved at a slightly lower level. The remaining 36 percent showed low involvement in the marital relationship; their satisfaction was low and in many cases declining. Among the women in the study, about half were no longer married (most due to widowhood);

another quarter were husband centered; and about 17 percent showed low involvement in their marriages. As compared with over one third of the husbands who reported low marital satisfaction, only one quarter of the wives did. These figures for women are merely suggestive, since the descriptions did not separate the women still married from the rest of the women studied. There was no evidence that these aging parents who had been married over forty years patterned their lifestyles in ways that were either responsive to or reciprocal to those of their spouses. The way they organized their lives seemed to be remarkably independent of each other (Maas and Kuypers, 1974, pp. 76–77). Thus, many of these more advantaged couples had different, perhaps less involved, marriages than the lower-middle-class couples studied by Lowenthal and her colleagues.

In general, one may conclude that for the happily married older couple, marriage is central to the "good life." It is a source of great comfort and support as well as the focal point of everyday life, and happily married couples can experience an increasing closeness as the years go by. In addition, there can be a high degree of interdependence in such couples, particularly in caring for each other in times of illness. The older husbands who believe they are happily married are particularly likely to view their wives as indispensable pillars of strength. For people in these happy marriages, widowhood can be a dismal prospect indeed, as will be discussed in the next chapter.

In a rare study that looked at economic factors, Hutchison (1975) found that being married made no difference to people whose income was below the poverty line, either in worrying, feeling lonely, or reporting unhappiness or dissatisfaction with their lives. On the other hand, if their income was just above the poverty line, married people were less likely to report these problems than people who were not currently married. Apparently, if one is below the poverty line, not even being married will help.

One key finding about happy marriages is that they tend to be characterized by a much greater equality between the partners than is true of unhappy older couples. This is brought about especially by a gradual loss of boundaries between sex roles and a decreasing division of household labor along male/female sex roles (Clark and Anderson, 1967, pp. 237–41).

While most older couples are happily married, a few are filled with hostility. Some feel that their husbands or wives are the cause of all their troubles, and they often wish that they could somehow terminate their marriages. Religious orthodoxy, such as the strong Catholic policy against divorce, has no doubt kept many such couples together who otherwise would have separated. The same could be said of social pressure in the community: The stigma of divorce has kept people together for years under a more or less armed truce. What is particularly disturbing is that many of these unhappy older people simply cannot cope with the increased demands that illness generates for the old (Clark and Anderson, 1967).

Generally, when both husband and wife become feeble, their sharing of work is on an idiosyncratic or "each does what he can" basis. The reciprocity between them becomes so intimate that the term *symbiotic* seems appropriate (Clark and Anderson, 1967; Cumming and Henry, 1961). In fact, when one partner dies, the other rarely survives.

Much of the research suggests that three themes dominate the general interactions of old couples: decrease in passion, increase in conventionality, and concern with health.

Divorce

So far, historical changes in sex roles do not seem to override the changes in marital satisfaction attributable to the duration of the relationship. It is true that divorce rates have risen, but there is no noteworthy increase in divorce rates after age forty and no clear-cut trend indicating change in the timing of divorce. Census data for 1972–1974 show that the average divorce occurs after six or seven years of marriage. If we look at separation instead of legal divorce, the pattern is one of highest rates within the first few weeks of marriage. Only the frequency of divorce has changed, not the age profile. More people of all ages now see it as an option.

Every year, nearly 10,000 Americans sixty-five or over are divorced. While this does not imply a new peaking of divorce in later life, it suggests that older couples are not immune to the tenor of the times, which makes divorce almost imperative for unhappy marriages. In fact, we may have reached a "tipping point," a reversal in general attitudes, where there is a general belief that marriages that are not happy should be terminated. Where once couples felt obligated to stay together even if they were highly incompatible and unhappy, and were ashamed if they did divorce, now such couples could feel apologetic if they *don't* divorce. While a number of family researchers suspect that many divorces may cause more problems than they solve, at present there is no sign that the divorce rate is decreasing.

Factors Influencing Marital Satisfaction

If we can presume from these ambiguous data that at least some couples experience a midlife decline in marital satisfaction, how can we account for it? A few possible explanations have been offered:

The Effect of Children

It is clear from almost all research on the effect of children upon their parents' marriage that the birth of the first child has a significantly depressing effect upon the marital relationship (LeMasters, 1957; Bohannon, 1971; Feldman, 1961; Lowenthal et al., 1975; Hoffman, 1978). Bohannon has said that middle-class Americans, unlike people in some other societies, establish a sort of antithesis between *parenting* and *spousing*. Although the middle-aged San Franciscans studied by Lowenthal and her colleagues held highly familistic values—they believed in being married and having children—and greatly appreciated their children, the disruptive influence of teenage children was a recurrent theme in their interviews. Feldman's (1964) control sample of childless couples did not show the same lowering of marital satisfaction over time that his group of parents did. Those women in the San Francisco sample who had prolonged their motherhood role as a primary focal point in their lives tended to have more troubles than those who turned to other interests (Spence and Lonner, 1971). Similar findings have been reported by Bart (1971), who used the vivid phrase *Mother Portnoys* to describe these women who had put "all their eggs in one basket" and ended up the most prone to a midlife depression. Even though most women do not see the empty nest as a crisis but a chance for greater freedom and opportunity (Lowenthal and Chiriboga, 1972; Neugarten, 1968), they too demonstrate the constricting effect of children.

We have said that the research in this whole area is contradictory, and the empty nest data are no exception. One woman in the San Francisco sample suggested that the empty nest is surrounded by telephone wires. Others have said, "What empty nest?" Their children continue to hang around in fact even though they have moved out in theory. A study of newlyweds by Ryder (1968) found that although some newlyweds do have little contact with their parents, others visit and telephone often and still use their parents' closet space, checking and charge accounts, car, and so on. We will discuss the subject of intergenerational relations in the next chapter at more length; here let it suffice to say that adult children can continue to influence their parents' marriages.

Individual Development

In an earlier chapter, we pointed out that there is more than one way to view the family over time. While we can focus on the individual members, in this case the husband or wife (or father and mother), we could also shift our focus to the couple as a system. Pineo (1961) explained the decrease in intimacy and satisfaction over twenty years of marriage—the increase in disenchantment—in terms of the degree of *fit* between the husband and wife. Since in our society marriage is the product of personal choice, and since presumably those who decide to marry feel that the person they choose is the best match they can get, marriage must logically begin at the point of maximal fit. This means that any change in either partner is likely to decrease the amount of fit—unless they are lucky enough to change in such ways as to maintain or increase their congruence. Table 3.4 diagrams the possible ways in which each spouse might change: to become more or less complex, such as toward more or less self-actualization, or to stay the same, and the effect upon their match of such change or lack of change. According to this model, if both husband and wife remain stable in personality over the years of their marriage (upper left cell of Table 3.4), their match can remain good. This may not be apparent while their children are present, because since the fit was just between the two of them, the children would disrupt it. After the children leave (or at least become somewhat less intrusive), however, the original good match can shine through. Incidentally, in other kinds of societies, where marriages are arranged by extended families for the benefit of the larger unit, the couple relationship might even be enhanced by the arrival and presence of children.

In the middle-diagonal cell of Table 3.4, both husband and wife develop toward greater complexity over time. Only if they both develop "on the same wave length" can their fit remain good—or perhaps even improve. However, there is danger that they will grow apart instead of together. In fact, those who are able to grow in unison may be rare exceptions. The same conclusions may be drawn for couples who decrease in complexity or deteriorate over time (lower

Table 3.4.   Possibilities for Husband-Wife Matching over Years of
Marriage as a Function of Personality Development in Either or Both

Development of Husband	*Development of Wife*		
	None (stable)	*Becomes More Complex*	*Becomes Less Complex*
None (stable)	Match should remain good. Perhaps dormant while children intervene, but, when they leave, may get "second honeymoon."	Match deteriorates. Wife's needs no longer met.	Match deteriorates. Husband's needs no longer met.
Becomes More Complex	Match deteriorates. Husband's needs no longer met.	Relationship has chance to develop if individuals' changes are on same path. But they could each develop in different directions and would no longer match.	Match deteriorates. Husband's needs no longer met.
Becomes Less Complex	Match deteriorates. Wife's needs no longer met.	Match deteriorates. Wife's needs no longer met.	Relationship has chance of staying matched if negative developments of both are synchronous; could be like "cooling off." But if not, synchronization will disappear.

Source: Troll, 1975.

right cell). If they deteriorate in the same way (for example, both "cool off"), they may remain well matched.

The same process of decreasing fit could come about by any kind of individual change process in husband and wife. For example, Neugarten and Gutmann (1968) found shifts in personality during the middle and later years that were associated with perceptions of ability to control one's own destiny. In their responses to a TAT-like picture, most young men—up to the age of the fifties—and some young women approached life from an orientation of *active mastery*. They felt that if they wanted something, it was up to them to go out and try to get it. During their fifties, there was a shift (though it should be remembered that these data are cross-sectional) toward *passive mastery* on the part of most men and some women. This was accompanied by feelings that they were not as powerful as they once thought but more like puppets of the larger forces outside them. Therefore, if they wanted something, they must fit in with these outside forces, placate or manipulate them, rather than oppose or ignore them. While most of the men in this period were becoming correspondingly more introspective and inner-oriented, most of the women the same age were becoming more comfortable with their assertiveness and were essentially moving in the opposite direction—toward more active mastery. These opposing shifts could lead toward androgyny on both sides, and require a renegotiation of a marital relationship. In old age, ten or twenty years later, both men and women tended to shift toward *magic mastery*. They distorted reality so as to feel they were still powerful. This may also require some re-negotiation.

There are other ways to apply a systemic point of view. For example, one could say that a system can react to change in one of four ways (Troll, 1975): It can deny it; it can alter just enough to return to equilibrium or a *homeostatic* status; it can fragment and fall apart; or it can "develop." Thus: (1) In spite of changes in a husband or wife, or in any strategic part of the situation in which they interact, the marriage could continue as if there had been no changes. For example. a couple whose children were adults and living in their own homes could continue to focus their relationship on their children and their pre-empty-nest roles as if the children were still small, living in the parental household, and in need of a great deal of parental care. (2) The marriage could change just a little. For example, a husband and wife could act toward each other as if they were the children who had left, treating each other with extra nurturance and protectiveness. (3) The marriage can fragment and end in divorce or alienation between spouses—marriages do exist in which one partner has not talked to the other for years. Or (4) the marriage could improve in any of a number of ways.

Not only would this imply a second honeymoon, but an even richer relationship than during the honeymoon, based on the more mature personalities of both spouses.

Health Factors in Marital Relations

Concern with health seems to come to the fore in the middle years. Axelson (1960) found this particularly true of the women in his sample of several hundred parents of newly married children, although Neugarten et al. (1963) report that it seems to be their husbands' health that middle-aged women are concerned about rather than their own. They do not want to be propelled into widowhood before their time. Feldman's (1964) older couples talked a lot about health. The research of Neugarten et al. (1963) on middle-aged women's attitude toward the menopause found no evidence for direct concern about this event in "normal" women—that is, those who were married and mothers and had not had a hysterectomy. The one hundred Chicago women they tested and interviewed declared that the biological change of menopause was, indeed, unpleasant, but that it soon passed and was followed by more pleasant conditions—greater freedom, better health than before, and greater life satisfaction. It is possible, therefore, that a woman's concern about health at this age is more what Neugarten calls a *rehearsal for widowhood,* or anticipatory socialization (Deutscher, 1962; Neugarten, 1968). As discussed elsewhere in this book, wives have real reason to be concerned; the consequences of having to nurse a husband or of becoming widowed are both unpleasant.

Role Strain

Both the number and intensity of social roles increase until the middle years; they start to decrease following retirement. Thus, Rollins and Cannon (1974) conclude that "role strain would be greatest at both ends of the family life cycle" (p. 281). These authors apparently end that cycle with the launching of children. Both men and women seem to find midlife a time of heightened role stress. Middle-class, middle-aged men are usually at the height of their occupational career and involved with its direct and adjunct activities. Working-class men are concerned with keeping their jobs and shoring up money for impending retirement. While some women are facing a gradually shrinking circle of intimate relationships in middle age (Lopata, 1977), most are expanding in many new ways, returning to work and school or to a variety of *recreative* activities (Troll et al., 1977). Table 3.3 shows

Table 3.5.   Labor Force Participation Rates by Age and Sex, 1970

Age	*Women*	*Men*	*Ratio*
	(percent)		*Women/Men*
45–54	54	93	.58
55–64	43	82	.52
65 and over	9	26	.35
70 and over	5	17	.29

Source: Miller, 1978.

labor force participation by age and sex. Women are still way behind men at any age, but it must be noted that over half of all middle-aged women held jobs in 1970. This means, for most women, that they have added a job outside the home to their continued work responsibilities inside the home.

Not only is role strain likely to be highest in middle age, it is also likely to be greater for women than for men. In part, this is due to sex-differentiated personality characteristics. Women are socialized or predisposed to be more *tuned in* to other people. They take on the concerns not only for their own work responsibilities but also for their husbands' jobs. We mentioned earlier that they also are the ones concerned about their husbands' health. As the family kin-keepers, they are also the ones who keep in touch with and worry about and help out their children, their parents, and their husbands' parents. The term *Cassandra syndrome,* discussed in Chapter 2, can be used to symbolize middle-aged women's "work of worry" (Troll and Turner, 1976).

Attachment Versus Attraction

Troll (Troll and Smith, 1976) has postulated that there is a fundamental inverse relationship between *attraction* and *attachment*. Attraction is high in the beginning of a new relationship, but attachment is low. Over the years, attraction wanes as novelty wanes, but attachment increases. Where marital satisfaction or happiness is measured in terms of attraction, a steady decrease over time would be inevitable, with perhaps a temporary rise when the children's leaving creates a new situation for husband and wife, and a possible restructuring of their relationship. The study by Reedy (1977) mentioned earlier found that couples married a short time said that love was very important; those married many years said that loyalty was more important.

Household Division of Labor

The influx of women into the labor market, together with increasing demand for equality in marriage, has led to renewed interest in the distribution of household work between husband and wife. Unfortunately, the data are fraught with errors. For one thing, the kinds of tasks that have been looked at, repeating those used by Blood and Wolfe (1960) in their classic study of marriage, do not adequately represent essential household work. A second problem is that reports of husbands' participation given by their wives are not consistent with husbands' own reports and, what is worse, with actual time-motion studies (Walker, 1970). Thus, while Bahr (1973) concluded that husbands of employed wives performed significantly more household tasks than husbands of full-time homemakers, Walker's data show that husbands spend one and a half hours per day in household work compared with five hours per day for employed wives. All studies agree that wives are responsible for and actually perform almost all janitorial services, child-care tasks, and meal preparation. Husbands are responsible for and generally perform a very few "masculine" tasks that, in any case, occur less frequently: minor repairs, shoveling snow, and mowing the grass. Emptying the garbage is an exception. Most studies do not even consider kin-keeping functions of wives such as visiting, keeping contact with, and writing to all geographically distant relatives (and friends). Over the life course, there is somewhat more sharing of household work before the first child is born and greater specialization following the first child (Hoffman, 1978). While data on earlier cohorts showed increasing role specialization over the years, more recent research (Kerckhoff, 1966a, b) does not. In an ongoing longitudinal study of retired couples, researchers are finding a great deal of sharing of household tasks. Although there is often a division of labor between husband and wife, the division is not made upon sex-stereotyped lines. The same kind of patterns are found among aging blacks as well as whites (Jackson, 1972a). If newer cohorts of more androgynous couples keep a more sharing relationship over time, balanced household and job responsibilities might persist into their later years. So far, such relationships are relatively infrequent even in younger couples (DeFrain, 1977). Lipman (1961, 1962) found that many retired husbands worked together with their wives in chores that required little specialized skill and knowledge, such as washing dishes and shopping for groceries. However, when Ballweg (1967) compared retired husbands with employed husbands of the same age, they were not more likely to share activities as a whole but to assume responsibility for a few tasks already socially defined as masculine. Since almost all older (and younger) adults in our society dislike housework, especially men and college-educated women, and since this trend is increasing, we are likely to find that less housework will actually get done, that standards for cleanliness will decrease, or that new forms of living will be favored which will minimize the need for housework.

Sexuality

The whole question of *sexuality* in the later years of marriage has not been studied adequately (see the review by Huyck, 1977). While there is evidence for decline in sexual activity (Masters and Johnson, 1968) during the middle years, much of this has been attributed to boredom. Neubeck (1969) and Cuber and Harroff (1965) talk about extramarital relations which serve to revive sexual interest, but the little evidence available suggests that most sexual experience takes place between marriage partners, and that most couples continue to enjoy sex into advanced old age.

In summarizing the changes in sexual physiology, Weg (1975) notes that interest and capacity persist through old age when a suitable mate is available. Past experience (enjoyment, frequency, and pleasure) are important predictors for sexual activity in later life ("use it or lose it"). Huyck (1977) concurs that whatever sexual patterns exist during the middle years are likely to persist into the later years. On the other hand, there are a few women who discover their own sexuality only in their late middle years. Those older women who do not do so may be the "good" girls of yesteryear who have now grown old, aver Datan and Rodeheaver (1977). Lowenthal and her associates (1975) found that one third of the preretirement group of husbands and wives (in their fifties and sixties) reported increasing sexual enjoyment since their children had left home, but half of the men and one third of the women experienced declining satisfaction in sexual relations in these years. Obviously, there are wide individual differences which may be related more to value systems and opportunity than to physical capacity. On the side of optimism is the reverse statistic that half of the men and two thirds of the women found their sexual experiences remaining at least as good as before, if not improving.

According to Feldman (1964) and others (Dentler and Pineo, 1960; Reedy, 1977; Westley and Epstein, 1960, 1961), sexual factors play a secondary role in marital adjustment in later years. This is consistent with the findings of a Carnegie study of 25,000 cases seen by marriage counselors in England (Brayshaw, 1962). For those married less than three years, sexual problems constitute 40 percent of the presenting symptoms, with living conditions and parental influence next. Ill health, the fourth reason, supplies only 14 percent of the cases. On the other hand, for those married over eighteen years, ill health is the first reason, accounting for 29 percent of the cases. Next are infidelity and incompatibility. Sex is the fourth reason, and accounts for only 15 percent of the cases. Not only do the reasons appear in different priorities, but the younger marriages tend to peak more around the first few reasons, while the older marriages find trouble in many areas about equally.

The findings of Masters and Johnson (1968) on sexual performance and sex drive in the later years of marriage is in general accord with the earlier findings of Kinsey (Kinsey et al., 1948, 1953). Adjusted women show no abatement of sex drive—but then, many women are not adjusted. Also, there is an ongoing attrition in the male sex drive, and if a woman is married to an older man, the effects of his diminished sexuality are relatively greater. While male sexual responsiveness is much diminished after sixty, part of this decrease is secondary impotence, which is reversible if such factors as monotony, an understanding partner, concern with economic pursuits, mental or physical infirmities can be controlled. Feigenbaum et al. (1966) found older men (ages sixty-two through ninety-six) more positive about sex than older women in their San Francisco community sample ($N = 273$), though higher socioeconomic status and more education were also associated with more positive interest in sex at this advanced age. Rubin (1965, 1968) states that the sexless older years are a self-fulfilling prophecy. Although there is no study of sexual behavior and sexual attitudes of older people on a good sample, enough data are available to conclude that there is no universal age cut-off point for sex. Clark and Anderson (1967) say that sex beyond age eighty is rare, however. The picture may change for future cohorts of old couples. Since there is currently greater concern with sexual satisfaction of both marriage partners, as well as greater acceptance of some alternate forms of sexual expression, more future couples may continue sexuality into late life.

Fertility has often been confused with sexuality. Thus it is folklore among many cultures that women lose their sexual interest and capacity at the time that they stop being fertile—at the menopause. Fertility declines in middle age for both sexes due to gonadal deterioration. It stops comparatively abruptly in women with the menopause, which occurs on the average in their early fifties. It continues longer, at a lowered level, in men, who reach their climacteric five or ten years later than women, and do so in a more gradual way. Because the male climacteric is less noticeable, it has less effect on behavior.

In both cross-sectional (Kinsey et al., 1948, 1953; Masters and Johnson, 1966) and longitudinal research (Pfeiffer et al., 1968), older men report greater interest and more activity in heterosexual intercourse than do older women. Among men, the median age of stopping intercourse was sixty-nine; among women, it was sixty. On the other hand, the longitudinal data show that about one quarter of the men and a few of the women experience not declining but rising sexual interest and activity with advancing age. It was noted earlier that much impotence and frigidity is attributable to extraneous factors. This can become exacerbated if a man, fearing any further failures to "perform," avoids sexual approaches to or by his wife. She can conclude that he no longer loves her or has found another woman. Mutual recrimination and alienation can follow. Or the middle-aged woman, similarly frustrated, can use the traditional excuse of menopause and turn away the sexual advances of her husband.

Retirement

The studies of the effects of retirement on marriage have centered primarily on the *division of household tasks* (Ballweg, 1967; Kerckhoff, 1964, 1966b) and concomitant *changes in sex role differentiation* (Lipman, 1960, 1961, 1962). These studies generally show a shift away from *expressive* behavior on the wife's part to mutually expressive behavior. That is, the husband shifts from the instrumental role of *good provider* to the more expressive role of *helping in the house,* while his wife moves from a relatively less expressive *good homemaker* to a more expressive *loving and understanding* role. The retired husband ends up sharing in household tasks, but whether or not he feels good about it seems to depend on his value system. If, as is true of many working-class husbands, "woman's work" is considered demeaning, the man sharing it feels devalued. This does not seem to be as common among middle class men.

Fengler (1975) studied wives' attitudes toward their husbands' retirement. His sample fell into three roughly equal categories: optimists (39%), neutralists (29%), and pessimists (32%). The optimists saw retirement as a time for an exciting new life together, one characterized by more companionship and shared activities. The neutralists expected retirement to change their marriage very little. The pessimists tended to fear that their husbands would find themselves with too much time on their hands and would intrude into their own domestic domains.

Kerckhoff (1966b) found that husbands do indeed experience greater involvement in household tasks after retirement, and that this change tends to be welcomed by the wives of men with middle- and upper-status jobs but not by wives of men with lower-status jobs. In another study, working-class women felt sorry that their husbands had retired (Heyman and Jeffers, 1968). If, as often happens, a husband retires because of poor health, it would not be surprising if this had an adverse effect on their marriage. Maas and Kuypers (1974) found no evidence that retirement as such created marital problems for middle-class husbands.

Remarriage

Not all older couples have to make the transition into retirement. Some marriages are started only after the partners are already retired. In 1970, over 45,000 older Americans married. About 5 percent of these were first-time marriages; the rest were remarriages (National Center for Health Statistics, 1974). Three quarters of those who remarried were widows and widowers and a quarter had been divorced at the time of remarriage.

The factors involved in marrying in later life are numerous, but two of the most important are *income* and the *sex ratio*. Before older people will marry, there generally has to be enough money between them to support their marriage. This is a limiting factor, particularly for lower-income men, who find it difficult to find a marriage partner unless they can bring their share of financial support to the union. Most pension and social security regulations inhibit remarriage because of their restrictive regulations.

The other factor is the excess of older women to older men. Because older men are vastly outnumbered by women of their own age, and because men tend to marry women younger than themselves, older men always have a much larger field to choose from compared with women. Among all people over sixty-five, there are about seventy-five men to one hundred women. It is not surprising, therefore, that in 1970 older grooms outnumbered older brides two to one. Among *unmarried* older people, there are about fifty men to every one hundred women. Of the 31,000 older men who got married in 1970, 59 percent married women under sixty-five, whereas of the 15,000 older women who married in 1970, only 15 percent married men under sixty-five. The sexual imbalance is dramatically reflected in the marriage rates: 15.6 per 1,000 per year for men over sixty-five, and 2.4 per 1,000 per year for women over sixty-five. A happy remarriage may ease the pain of widowhood or divorce, but this option simply is not available to most middle-aged or older women.

In a study of one hundred couples who married in later maturity, McKain (1969) found that companionship was by far the most frequently given reason for remarriage. Previous good experience with marriage helped. Few of the couples he interviewed believed in romantic love. Besides companionship, they wanted lasting affection and regard. As McKain (1969, p. 36) stated, "The role of sex in the lives of these older people extended far beyond love-making and coitus; a woman's gentle touch, the perfume of her hair, a word of endearment—all these and many more reminders that he is married help to satisfy a man's urge for the opposite sex. The same is true for the older wife." A few older people remarried to allay their anxiety about poor health. As discussed earlier, it is likely these were men looking for a nurse/wife. Single older women complain that the men they meet are just looking for a nurse—"and who needs that?" (Troll and Turner, 1976). Some remarried to avoid having to depend on children.

Many older people tended to select mates who reminded them of a previous spouse (McKain, 1969). In fact, many married people they had known for many years, often as part of an earlier couples group that included their spouses. For example, a widower would marry a widow who had been part of the same social group when their wife and husband, respectively, were living. They thus followed the same pattern of *homogamy* as young couples, marrying those from similar backgrounds in socioeconomic status, religion, ethnicity, education, and even personality. About three fourths of older new marriages include widowed people (Treas and Van Hilst, 1976). Widows may be preferred to divorced people, although in this age group there are probably more altogether who are widowed than divorced.

Using such unobtrusive measures as displays of affection, respect and consideration, obvious enjoyment of each other's company, lack of complaints about each other, and pride in their marriage as indicators of successful marriage, McKain found that these indices were more common among couples who had known each other well over a period of years. Probably the prime reason that long friendship was so strongly related to successful remarriage in later life is that intimate knowledge allowed better matching of interests and favorite activities.

Approval of the marriage by family and friends was important for the success of these marriages, as it is in earlier life (McKain, 1969). Many older couples face considerable social opposition to marriage. There is a belief that they do not *need* to be married since marriage is primarily a reproductive and childrearing institution. Their children may also be concerned about what might happen to the estate. Since older people generally share the beliefs of their generation, they are often very sensitive to this pressure, and encouragement from children and friends can be strategic.

There also appears to be an element of *personal adaptability* to life changes in general which influences adjustment to retirement marriage. McKain found that unless both the bride and groom were reasonably well-adjusted individuals, marriage in later life was not likely to be successful. Financial factors were also important. It helped if both partners owned homes, for example. In part, the importance of dual home ownership was symbolic, indicating that each partner brought something concrete to the marriage. The same principle applied if both had sufficient income. Arrangements for pooling property or giving to children were similarly symbolic, indicating the priority a partner held in the eyes of the other. Where the marriage partner had priority over children in the distribution of resources, the marriage was more likely to be successful.

Summary

We can conclude from the research to date, scanty as it may be, that marriage and sexuality remain important to people throughout life. While husband/wife relations are susceptible to health and economic conditions, and to presence or absence of children in the home, they tend to be sources of enjoyment to older people, particularly during the post-childrearing period. Information about division of household work is contradictory. Apparently some couples share this much more than others, some along sex-stereotyped lines, some not. More older couples get divorced than formerly, but this seems to be part of the historically shifting attitudes and tendencies toward divorce more than age-related events. There is no evidence for peaking of divorce in middle age, and it is still most frequent at the beginning of marriage. Remarriage is much more common for older men than for older women, probably because of the greater availability of women than of men.

Chapter Four

On Being Unmarried in Later Life

While most people are married during their middle and even later years, a substantial number, especially women, are not. This chapter considers the influence of not being married on the experiences of the later years of life. *Widowhood** is the main way people become single in later life, but we also will consider those who get divorced or separated and those who never marry.

Widowhood

Our discussion of widowhood will begin with the prevalence of widowhood in later life and then will consider bereavement, and the impact of widowhood on relations with family and friends. We will also identify some differences by social class, racial and ethnic groups, and sex.

Prevalence

For women past fifty, widowhood is usually a permanent status, though not necessarily a preferred one. Only 5 percent of women who become widowed after fifty-five ever remarry (Cleveland and Gianturco, 1976). This is in contrast to widowers, most of whom remarry if they are under seventy. It is this sex difference, based in

---

*Generally we use the term *widowhood* to refer to both men and women.

part upon sex differences in life expectancy (which are increasing) and in part upon the custom for men to marry younger women, which makes it much easier for men to remarry in old age than for women to do so. As can be seen in Table 4.1, there are thus many more older men who have a wife than older women who have a husband.

Bereavement

Widowhood usually begins with a period of mourning or *bereavement,* followed by gradual adjustment to the new status as well as to the loss. If dying has been prolonged, of course, much of the mourning process may have preceded actual death and the post-death grieving process, though just as acute, may be curtailed. In any event, there is wide variation in the duration of acute grief; it may be brief or it may be lengthy. In Lopata's (1973) Chicago study of widows, 48 percent said they were over their husband's death within a year, while 20 percent said they had never gotten over it and did not expect to.

Bereavement, like most reactive depressions, can take a variety of forms: physical, emotional, intellectual, or any combination of these. Common physical reactions include shortness of breath, frequent sighing, tightness in the chest, feelings of emptiness in the abdomen, loss of energy, lack of muscular strength, or digestive disorders (Kalish, 1976). These reactions are particularly frequent immediately

Table 4.1.   Marital Status by Age: United States, 1975

	Male				Female			
Marital Status	55 to 64 Years	65 to 74 Years	75 Years and Over	65 Years and Over	55 to 64 Years	65 to 74 Years	75 Years and Over	65 Years and Over
Percent, total	100.0	100.0	100.0	100.0	100.0	100.0	100.0	100.0
Single	6.5	4.3	5.5	4.7	5.1	5.8	5.8	5.8
Married	85.0	83.9	70.0	79.3	69.3	49.0	23.4	39.1
Spouse present	81.8	81.8	68.2	77.3	66.7	47.3	22.3	37.6
Spouse absent	3.2	2.0	1.8	2.0	2.6	1.8	1.1	1.5
Widowed	4.0	8.8	23.3	13.6	20.3	41.9	69.4	52.5
Divorced	4.5	3.1	1.2	2.5	5.3	3.3	1.5	2.6

Source: U.S. Bureau of the Census, 1976, p. 46.

following the death and generally diminish with time. That these are real physical upsets is suggested by the finding that average mortality rates of recently widowed people are slightly higher than those still married. There is some evidence, however, that this differential may disappear after about five years (Maddison and Viola, 1968; Parkes et al., 1969).

Emotional reactions can include anger, guilt, sadness, anxiety, and preoccupation with thoughts of the dead spouse (Parkes, 1972). These responses also tend to diminish with time. The connection between emotional and physical reactions is suggested by such findings as those of Bornstein et al. (1973), whose longitudinal study of widows and widowers showed that those who became depressed during the bereavement period were likely to report a disproportionately higher level of poor health a year later than those who did not report depression.

Intellectual reactions include *sanctifying* the memory of the dead spouse. In this process, his or her negative characteristics are forgotten, leaving only a positive, idealized memory. Somehow we think it wrong to speak ill of the dead. But widows not only don't speak ill, they truly don't think ill and even tend to exaggerate or make up good qualities. Lopata (1973) reports that even women who hated their husbands thought that the statement, "My husband was an unusually good man," was true. Such idealization of the dead can have positive value in that it satisfies survivors' needs to believe that each life has some meaning. On the other hand, it could interfere with the formation of new intimate relationships (Lopata, 1973); if one's dead spouse was so ideal, no living human can match him or her.

Glick et al. (1974) found that men and women react somewhat differently to bereavement. Men more often feel they have lost part of themselves, while women more often feel deserted and abandoned. On the other hand, men find it more difficult to express their grief; they also accept the reality of the death somewhat more quickly than women do.

There are various ways in which others help the widowed person. In the first few days, they are excused from many responsibilities. They are not expected to go to their jobs. Family (usually sisters or daughters) and friends help with cooking and caring for children or other dependents. The men (usually brothers or sons) take care of many of the funeral and financial arrangements. Adult children often make decisions for older women. But such social supports tend to be temporary, lasting a few weeks at most.

Consequences of Widowhood

As mentioned earlier, higher death rates among men and higher marriage rates among widowers result in five widows to every widower among older people (Miller, 1978). Thus, we often think of widowhood as something that happens mainly to women. Yet in 1975, almost one fourth of the men over seventy-five were widowed (and not remarried). This proportion has been decreasing recently, however. Since it is reasonable to assume that losing a spouse is a different experience for women and men, we will examine these two situations separately.

Women.   In American society, the role of widow is a long-term one, particularly for older women. Actually, young widows are soon considered single again rather than widows (Lopata, 1973). Because young widows are so much in the minority among their age peers, they tend to feel stigmatized. In contrast, older women see widowhood as more normal. Even as early as sixty-five, a third of all women are widows. Thus, the prevalence of widowhood in later life combines with low expectations for remarriage to produce a more definite social position for the older widow.

Even so, the role of older widow is a vague one. Ties with their husband's family may be drastically reduced, yet they are supposed to be interested in keeping his memory alive. They are also not supposed to be interested in men but to associate primarily with other widows or with their children (Lopata, 1973).

Being a widow changes the basis of *self-identity* for those women for whom the role of wife and mother is central, having structured their lives not only in their households but also on the job. In answering the question, "Who am I?" such women would usually have put *wife of* at the top of their list, but many find it harder to do the same with *widow of.* They have also lost the person who supported their self-definition. Husbands who were best friends and confidants may have been very important in making them feel that they were good persons. It is not uncommon for older widows to "consult" their dead husbands about whether they are "doing the right thing" ten years after they died.

Lopata (1973) found that widows cope with this identity crisis in different ways. Role-oriented women can turn to other roles, taking a job or increasing their investment in a job they already have. They may also become more involved in civic or social organizations. Those who need confirmation of their personal qualities may become more involved with friends and family, although in a later study Lopata

(1977) found that those widows who had not had friends outside the family before their husband died did not tend to acquire any after his death. Widows who base their identity on things rather than on people are often in trouble because they find that their income level is substantially reduced. All of these orientations may, of course, be present in the same person.

Women vary in the extent to which the role of wife is central to their identity. For many, the role of mother superseded the role of wife. Others had never developed a close, intimate relationship with their husbands. Such widows must then negotiate with their family and friends to gain acceptance in their own right rather than as their husband's wife.

Loneliness. The concept of *loneliness* is central to discussions of widowhood, divorce, and old age, although it is not always treated analytically. It is important to distinguish between living alone, feeling lonely, feeling isolated, feeling desolate, and so on. Many people—young and old—who live alone do not feel lonely, isolated, or desolate, and many people who live with a spouse or other relative do feel lonely, isolated, and desolate. Many widows quickly grow accustomed to living alone; more than half of older widows do so and apparently even prefer to do so. They miss their husbands both as persons and as partners in many activities (Lopata, 1973; Blau, 1961). However, and particularly if they are older, they become involved with friendship groups of other widows and tend to miss their husband's companionship less. In residential areas with a high concentration of older widows, loneliness is reported much less frequently than in areas where such widows are more isolated. In fact, Atchley, Pignatiello, and Shaw (1975) found that widows had higher rates of interaction than married older women. And Arling (1976) found that having strong relationships with friends and neighbors was more related to high morale among widows than were ties with family.

The amount and kind of *social disruption* caused by widowhood depends largely on what life activities had been shared with the husband. For example, middle-class women are more likely than working-class women to have seen themselves as part of a husband-wife team, so that their involvement in a wide variety of roles and activities would be impaired by their husband's death.

Widowhood has its most immediate impact on family roles. Contacts with in-laws are usually lost, for example, particularly if children are grown. Contacts with children usually increase for a time, but few move in with their children except as a last resort (Lopata, 1973), preferring "intimacy at a distance." First, they do not wish to become embroiled in conflict over managing the flow of household activity, and after being in charge of their own homes, it is hard for American widows to accept a subordinate position in another woman's house, especially a daughter-in-law's. Second, they do not want to be involved in the dilemmas of rearing children. They feel that they have done their work, raised their children, and deserve a rest (Lopata, 1973).

Patterns of mutual aid between children and parents are often altered, so that older widows usually grow closer to their daughters and more distant from their sons (Adams, 1968a, b). Because adult sons often feel responsible for their mothers' welfare and because older widows often want to be responsible for themselves, there is great potential for conflict and guilt in the older widow/son relationship. Relationships with the extended family (brothers, sisters, aunts, uncles, cousins, and so on) also change, increasing immediately after death but tapering off within a short time (Lopata, 1973).

The impact of widowhood on friendship depends on the proportion of the widow's friends who are also widows. If she is one of the first in her groups of friends to become widowed, she may find that her friends feel awkward about death and grief—they do not want to face what in all likelihood is their own future. If friendship groups consisted mainly of couples, then the widow may be included for a time, but she will probably feel out of place. The widow may also encounter jealousy on the part of still-married friends.

On the other hand, if the widow is one of the last to become widowed in a group of friends, she may find great comfort among friends who are familiar with her problems. In fact, as a group of women friends grows older, those who are still married may sometimes feel left out because their widowed friends do many things as a group that they do not feel free to join. For these people, widowhood brings the compensation of being among old friends again. In sum, widowhood is easier for older than for younger women.

Churches and voluntary associations organized around interests can provide avenues for increased social contact for widows, since these activities do not usually depend upon having a spouse or being accompanied by a member of the opposite sex. Women's groups are often more comfortable than heterosexual groups because they do not confront widows with being the lone single woman.

Social class is also a factor in adjustment to widowhood. Middle-class women are more likely than working-class women to have balanced their roles of wife and companion and mother. Therefore, the loss of comradeship can often be traumatic for them. On the other hand, middle-class women also tend to have more social options, more nonfamily friends, and more organizational activity, not to mention more personal resources in general. They usually have a more secure income, more education, and more job skills. To balance this in a small way, many working-class women tend to emphasize their mother role more than their wife role, and thus may experience less personal loss. But we must not forget that working-class women have fewer friends, fewer organizational memberships, less money, and fewer personal resources. On the whole, then, working-class widows are much more likely to be isolated and lonely than are middle-class widows.

Among low-income elderly, the widowed were consistently more negative in their self-reports of life satisfaction (Hutchison, 1975). In terms of economic impact on morale, widowhood is a more important factor among the low (but not lowest) than among those at the poverty level. At the poverty level, the grim problems of surviving tend to lessen the likelihood of emotional closeness between husband and wife. Furthermore, poverty often leads to lowered social participation outside the home (Atchley, 1975b). In fact, a five-country investigation of widowhood (Harvey and Bahr, 1974) found that the major long-term negative effects of widowhood were primarily associated with poverty.

Class differences are particularly large among blacks. Working-class black women tend to become widowed at even earlier ages than working-class whites. On the other hand, overt hostility between the sexes is more prevalent among blacks, and therefore widows sanctify their husband's memory less. As a result, widowhood brings less emotional distress among working-class blacks than among working-class whites (Lopata, 1973).

There also are considerable *ethnic* and *foreign-birth differences* in the impact of widowhood, though these are complex and vary with the kinds of expectations older women have been socialized for and the congruence between these expectations and the attitudes of younger generations in their family. Foreign-born widows are much more likely to have had the kind of traditional expectations for respect and care which entail greater identity problems when the younger members of their families were brought up to different values. For example, many foreign-born older women were reared in cultural traditions that offer widows a high degree of involvement with extended kin. To the extent that the younger extended kin and in-laws do not share this orientation, there is room for a greater gap between what the older foreign-born widow expects from her family and what she gets. A similar pattern prevails among older widows reared in some areas of Appalachia.

Men. The impact of widowhood on men has received little systematic attention. The literature on this subject is long on speculation and short on systematic research. Nevertheless, it is important to outline both what we do know and what we need to know about being a widower, as a guide for future research.

The role of widower is probably even vaguer than that of widow. Because widowers who have not remarried are not very common in the community until after age seventy-five, their common status does not solidify them into groups. Like widows, they are expected to preserve the memories of their wives and are not expected to show interest in other women (Berardo, 1968). Indications are that many widowers adhere to the former (Glick et al., 1974) but ignore the latter, as can be inferred from the remarriage rates cited earlier.

Because the male role traditionally emphasizes other roles in addition to that of husband, widowers are probably not as apt as widows to encounter an acute identity crisis when they lose their husband *role*. But, as mentioned earlier, men are more likely than women to see their spouse as an important part of *themselves* (Glick et al., 1974). In addition, older men are less likely than women to have a confidant other than their spouse (Powers et al., 1975), and thus can experience painful loneliness (Atchley, 1975b; Petrowsky, 1976; Bell, 1975).

How older men cope with widowhood's impact on their identity also probably depends, as older women's reactions do, on how the lost relationships fit into the men's *personal goal structures*. Despite current stereotypes about men's overinvolvement with their jobs, there is little evidence that widowhood is any less devastating for men than for women. In fact, it can wreck a man's concept of life in retirement completely. There is little basis for assuming that marriage is less important to older men than it is to older women.

So far, there has been limited study of the impact of widowhood on men's roles outside the household. Glick et al. (1974) report that widowers have more difficulty than widows with work during the mourning period. However, they do not differ from widows in isolation from kin or voluntary associations, nor are either widows or widowers more isolated than their married peers. In fact, those who have friends tend to see them more often (Petrowsky, 1976). When Atchley (1975c) controlled for social class, he found that widowhood tends to increase contacts with friends among middle-class widowers and decrease them among lower-class widowers. It could be that the large surplus of widows in senior centers and similar social groups for older people (generally used more by working-class than middle-class people) may inhibit the working-class widowers in developing new kinds of community participation. Such widowers tend to be embarrassed and even harassed by the competition among widows for their attention. But beyond this, they are unaccustomed to take the lead in such preponderantly female gatherings. While they may be nominally the leaders there, they are often frustrated and intimidated by the tendency of the women to dominate discussions and other activities.

Petrowsky (1976) found that widowers were much less involved in religious activities than were widows, but this is likely to be due to a continuation of sex differences in religious participation established earlier in life. Since Petrowsky's data are cross-sectional, we need longitudinal research to confirm this.

Very little has been written about age, social class, racial, or ethnic variations in the impact of widowhood on older men. Some of the variations noted for widows, however, no doubt apply to men as well. This area is greatly in need of research.

There is currently a controversy over whether widowhood is more difficult for older women or for older men. We mentioned earlier that age had a lot to do with reaction to widowhood. We must remember that it is more likely to occur in old age for men, and in middle age or later maturity for women. It is important, therefore, to compare widowers with widows of a similar age. Much of the research that has been done to date has not done this.

Some people feel that widowhood is more difficult for women. Some feel that it is more difficult for men. Berardo (1968, 1970) is the leading proponent of the idea that older men find widowhood more difficult than do older women. He suggests that men are ill-prepared to fend for themselves—to cook their own meals, keep house, and so on—and therefore end up having to give up their independent households. Berardo also feels that men have more difficulty finding a substitute source of intimacy. He says that courtship opportunities are limited for widowers and that friends and children see them as being too old for "that sort of thing." Berardo feels that widows have the advantage of continuing their role of housewife, a meaningful activity that provides continuing standards for behavior. He sees widows as being much more able to maintain an independent residence and at the same time more able to gain acceptance in the households of their children, should the need arise.

On the other side of this debate, Bell (1971) concluded that widowhood was harder on older women than on older men because: (1) being a wife is a more important role for women than being a husband is for men; (2) widows are given less encouragement to remarry; (3) widows face a bleaker financial future with fewer financial skills; (4) widows are more isolated because women are expected not to be socially aggressive; and (5) the lack of available men makes remarriage difficult for all but a few older widows. Recently, however, he has agreed that the problems of survivorship *are* greater for husbands (1975).

This controversy raises several issues in comparing widowers with widows. Between the ages of sixty-five and seventy-four, widowers in general are slightly more likely than widows to live in group quarters such as hotels or rooming houses rather than in independent households; after age seventy-five, there is little sex difference. Widowers who live in their own homes are slightly *more* likely to live alone than are widows. Thus, those men who remain widowers are not significantly less likely than widows to live alone.

Widowers are only slightly less likely than widows to be living with children. When they live in multiperson households, however, widowers are much more likely to be considered the household head.

Berardo made the usual assumptions that jobs are more important to men than to women and that retirement is an identity crisis primarily for men. He saw widowhood as a *cumulative role loss* only for men. Atchley (1975b) presents a somewhat different analysis. Since he found little evidence that leaving the job at retirement represented an identity crisis for large proportions of either men or women, he concluded that job loss is not a significant source of distress even in widowhood. He suggested that widowhood interacts with retirement to the extent that widowhood wrecks plans for a retirement lifestyle built around being a member of a couple. And this type of interaction between retirement and widowhood is probably as applicable to widows as to widowers.

But what about the housewife role? Berardo feels that the continuity of the housewife role is an advantage for widows. However, what is retained is the role of house*keeper*, not house*wife*. The widow loses the housewife role because widowhood and the empty nest take away her clients (Lopata, 1973). To some women, doing for oneself has less satisfaction than doing for others. There may also be a decrease in the time required for homemaking tasks.

Berardo feels that widowers have more difficulty than widows with finding alternate sources of intimacy because of social norms against courtships and remarriage for older men. But every year nearly 30,000 older widowers remarry, compared to about 15,000 older widows who remarry.

Widowers are much less likely than widows to have had a *confidant*—a very close friend—other than their wives. Therefore, widowers *need* remarriage more than widows do, in order to find a new confidant. As for the social discouragement of remarriage, McKain (1969) reports no sex difference in the extent to which children oppose remarriage, even though he does report that children's opposition is a significant obstacle to remarriage.

There can be little doubt that widows are far worse off financially than widowers, especially in the working class. In traditional marriages, the wife is usually ignorant of the family finances and has no training in how to manage money (Lopata, 1973). In addition, the incomes of widows average considerably less than the incomes of widowers. And Atchley's (1975b) research cited earlier suggests that this poverty is a critical factor for working-class widows.

Atchley (1975b) found that widowed older people were significantly more often lonely than married older people, and that working-class widowed older people were more often lonely than those in the middle class. He found no significant sex differences, however, in the prevalence of loneliness among the widowed. On the other hand, widowers were much more likely than widows to increase participation in organizations and contact with friends.

Thus, no aspect of widowhood appears demonstrably more difficult for older widowers than for older widows, but widows are clearly worse off than widowers in terms of finances and prospects for remarriage.

A Conceptual Limitation of Current Research

Most researchers study widowhood as a status rather than as a process. The result is that the short-term and long-term effects of widowhood are seldom identified. Miller (1977) has discussed this problem in relation to the economic adjustments of older women. We do not know whether economic problems might be cumulative during widowhood, with long-term widows having more severe economic problems than short-term widows, or whether there is a long-term recovery from a short-term crisis. Studying widows as a category without regard to duration may cloud attempts to clarify the process of economic adjustment to widowhood. We might assume that problems of morale and loneliness are more common in the early period of widowhood than later. Thus studies that do not differentiate long-term from short-term effects could minimize the problems of loneliness in widowhood. In many samples of widows, there are probably more long-term than short-term widows.

Divorced Older People

In 1975, less than 5 percent of people over fifty-five were currently divorced—and not remarried (see Table 4.1). However, about 11,000 older Americans get divorces each year. There has been very little research on the impact of divorce on older people or on the impact that being divorced may have on an older person's life. We do know that many women who are divorced are effectively deprived of income, and only recently has legal and political action been taken about *displaced homemakers*. Such women are not entitled to social security benefits unless they were married over twenty years, nor are they eligible for their ex-husband's private pension benefits. If they are not entitled to retirement benefits in their own right, they are forced to accept welfare. In a current study of the perceptions of income adequacy by women age fifty and over, Sheila Miller found that the divorced women felt much worse off than even the widows. This applies not only to financial matters but also to self-esteem and relations with others. Widowhood is more likely to be seen as a sad experience, divorce as a sinful or shameful one. Thus, widows could even increase in self-esteem and divorced people could decrease. In addition, divorce of older parents can be expected to have an impact on relations with adult children and other kin, who are often forced to take sides and may avoid both parents. This is one of the most neglected areas of research in social gerontology.

Sexuality of Widowed and Divorced
Older People

In today's cohorts of older people, sexual activity and sexual attitudes are generally *conservative* or *conventional* compared to those of many youth today. Older cohorts are primarily heterosexual in practice and limited to the conventional coital position (Huyck, 1977). Therefore, older women who lose their male partner in widowhood or divorce generally end all sexual activity. They say, "It needs a man." Because of the disproportion in the supply of opposite-sexed partners, older men may not face this problem. Furthermore, current thinking about differences in sexuality holds that women can continue to enjoy sex much longer than men, so that those men over seventy-five who do not remarry may no longer feel the need for sex. Such a conclusion must be viewed with caution, however, since sex is not coital alone (see discussion in Chapter 3). Later generations may find it easier to substitute masturbation or to try other kinds of sexual partners, but about this we can only speculate—even most youth of today still prefer "conventional" sex, after all.

Never-Married Older People

In 1975, less than 5 percent of older men and women in the United States had never been married. Although one might expect that they would be isolated and cut off from potential sources of help in old age, Clark and Anderson (1967, p. 256) did not find this to be true, at least in San Francisco. They found that, apparently because never-married people learned very early in life to cope with loneliness and to look after themselves, they were successfully autonomous and self-reliant in later years. Their independence and strengths may even have been factors in early life which encouraged them not to marry just for the sake of marrying. This would be particularly true of women (Bernard, 1973). Among the benefits, these "loners" are often spared the grief that comes from widowhood. Thus, while people who never marry may miss a lot of the "good" parts of life, they also seem to miss some of the "bad" (Gubrium, 1975).

Gubrium (1975) found that never-married older people tended to be life-long isolates who were not especially lonely in old age, since

their isolation was "normal." As Shanas et al. (1968) pointed out earlier, isolation is different from desolation. In short, it may be easier to
have never loved than to have loved and lost.

Most men stay unmarried because they want personal freedom
from involvement. The bachelor appears to be motivated by an intense
desire to escape the kind of involvement present in his family of orientation. The never-married older woman, on the other hand, often appears to be motivated by her desire to stay close to her family of
orientation and by her choice of career (this latter factor is becoming
less important because very few careers today require one to remain
unmarried).

Older people who never married might be expected to have
more contacts with extended kin than those who married. However,
Atchley, Pignatiello, and Shaw (1975) found that this depends a great
deal on social class, at least for women. Never-married older women
teachers interacted with extended kin significantly more than those
who were married. But among older telephone workers, those who
never married had much lower levels of interaction with extended family as compared to those who were married. In their total interaction
patterns, teachers appeared to compensate for being single by a dis-
proportionate involvement with relatives while telephone operators
tended to compensate by having relatively more contacts with nonre-
lated friends. Single older women who had been telephone company
employees had much lower overall interaction levels than married
women employees.

Summary

While a substantial number of older people are married and live
with their spouses, marriage or remarriage is progressively less available for aging women. Most older unmarried people today are thus
women who have been widowed. Because they are financially disadvantaged, particularly if they have been divorced, many of the negative
factors associated with not being married in later life are related to
income. In many ways, those who have never married seem to be
better off. They have learned to live alone and like it and do not suffer
some of the stress of losing a spouse. Older widows often turn to
friends for companionship and, if they are widowed late enough so that
most of their friends are, too, they may adjust well.

Chapter Five

Parents and Their Adult Children

Relationships between older parents and their adult children have been studied more extensively than most other topics in this book. Unfortunately, this statement does not mean that the research is adequate; it often raises more questions than it answers. This chapter begins with prevalence: How many older adults have living children? We will review research in five general indices of parent/child relationships: (1) residential proximity, (2) interaction frequency and type, (3) mutual aid, (4) family values, and (5) quality of relationships—intergenerational continuity and feelings.

Prevalence of Children

Between the ages of fifty-eight and sixty-three, over 80 percent of those who have ever married have living children (Murray, 1976). Roughly this same percentage is found in all surveys of older people. In a study of people sixty-five and over in seven countries, Shanas (1973) reported the same proportion, and so did Harris (1975) in a nationwide poll of Americans sixty-five and over. In fact, most older people who have no living children have never married. Thus, it is safe to say that the role of parent is possible for most Americans in the middle and older years. It is even more intriguing to realize that about 10 percent of those over sixty-five also have children who are over sixty-five. Finally, as we will see, most of these older Americans are not at all isolated from their adult children; they frequently play the role of older parent (or child of older parent).

As noted in Chapter 2, four general kinds of information are used in the analysis of parent/adult-child relationships: (1) *residential proximity*—how near they live to each other; (2) *interaction frequency and type*—how often they visit, phone, or write to each other; (3) *mutual aid*—whether it is in household services, gifts, or money; and (4) *feelings*, such as love or obligation as well as a variety of other subtle and qualitative indices such as valuing *familism, solidarity, attachment,* or *loyalty,* transmission of values (perhaps bilaterally), and intrinsic meaningfulness to each other.

It is clear that operational definitions of these indices will vary widely in specificity, simplicity, and objectivity. On one end will be discrete measures, such as number of miles or minutes apart, or number of times contacted per day or week. On the other end will be highly judgmental ratings of strength and kind of interpersonal bonds. Not only are these measurements of different orders, but the behaviors they measure, particularly the more qualitative aspects, can fluctuate, ebbing and flowing over the course of life or even from day to day or minute to minute. As more research becomes available in this area, we are likely to see that we need many measurements at the same time. One index alone will not pick up the complex aspects of close human relationships such as those involved in parent/child relationships that have endured over many years and many changes in both or all members involved.

Residential Proximity

Geographic distance is usually measured functionally rather than in absolute distance between households. For urban areas, a scale might be as follows: within the same household or apartment building, within the same block, within walking distance (not very far for an aged person), within a half-hour bus ride, within the city, within the metropolitan area, within several hours' drive (or one hundred miles), and outside convenient driving distance. Data on residential nearness have been collected by many investigators; at least twenty-five major surveys have been conducted (see Chapter 2 and Troll, 1971a for review).

Almost all these surveys show that older people prefer, whenever possible, to live in their own homes but near their children. This is particularly true if they (the parents) are married. In a recent tabulation of 1970 U.S. Census data (public use sample), 9 percent of those older people who live with a child are men and 81 percent are women. (Sex differences are discussed later in this section.) Murray (1976) found that currently nonmarried people between fifty-eight and sixty-three—a slightly younger group—were more likely to live with relatives other than children; this was particularly true for men. Moving in with children is an action taken only where there is not enough money to live alone, where health is so poor that self-care is impossible (as with very old parents), or—to a lesser extent—where a spouse has died. It is not a favored solution. Of people sixty-five and over who do live with their child, more are likely to live with an unmarried child than with a married one, more with a daughter (65 percent) than with a son (35 percent). In most of these cases, furthermore, it is the parent that tends to be the *head of household*, with the unmarried son or daughter moving in with parents—or remaining with parents—rather than older parents moving in with children. Finally, such joint households are usually two-generation, not three or more. Where the oldest generation moves in with a younger one, it is usually after the grandchildren have moved out. Fewer than 8 percent of American households are true three-generation ones, with grandchildren in them.

While joint households are the exception rather than the rule, related nuclear households tend to be near each other, particularly among urban working-class families (social class differences are reviewed later). Shanas et al. (1968), in a study of old people in three industrial societies, found that 84 percent of those over sixty-five lived less than an hour away from one of their children. Unfortunately, developmental comparisons are treacherous because data for somewhat younger families—for example, for middle-aged parents and their children—use different measurements. Adams (1968a) and Reiss (1962) both focus on the percent of *all known* relatives; Rosenberg (1970) focuses on the existence of primary and secondary kin within the city. Thus, it is hard to decide whether Adams's finding that one third of his young adults (average age about thirty-three) live near their parents compares with the figures of Shanas et al. (1968), who only asked about one child per parent (over sixty-five). It may be that there is a period in the life course—when parents are middle-aged and children are beginning their own family household—when the two generations are more geographically distant. This is suggested by the data of Willmott and Young (1960) and by Litwak (1960b). It seems to be particularly true for middle-class families. When the parents retire and grow older, though, they may migrate to be near one of their children (Bultena and Wood, 1969).

There is some evidence that people in their middle years may return to the geographic areas where they grew up (Lee, 1974). In addition, when older parents' need for aid in maintaining their household increases, there is a good possibility that some adult children move to be closer to their elderly parents. The topic of return migration in order to be closer to family has not been researched adequately. When Gray and Smith (1960) studied migrating families, for instance, one of their incidental findings was the prevalence of marital problems attributed to the separation of the wife from her relatives. More recent surveys have suggested that executives are more reluctant to move now, and moving companies have been reporting decreases in such company moving (*New York Times, 1975*).

Interaction Frequency

The findings on interaction among kin in the second half of life parallel those on residential proximity. Most older parents and middle-aged children see each other often. If, as in many middle-class families, they live too far apart for regular weekly visiting, they maintain contact by telephone and letter writing and then get together for extended visits.

Interaction has usually been measured by frequency of face-to-face visiting, though a few surveys also include telephoning and letter writing. Visiting has occasionally even been analyzed further along kinds of activities shared, such as talking, working together, rituals, and recreation. Almost as many investigators have studied interaction frequency as residential proximity (see review by Troll, 1971a).

In the Shanas et al. (1968) large-scale study of old people in three industrial countries (United States, England, and Denmark), 84 percent of the American respondents with living children had seen at least one of their children within the previous week, and 90 percent within the last month.

Among older parents not living with a child, Shanas (1973) found that 52 percent had seen a child within the last twenty-four hours and 78 percent had seen one within the last week. In Bracey's (1966) Louisiana sample, the comparable figures were 34 percent and 78 percent, respectively. Watson and Kivett (1976) reported that 90 percent of older fathers had seen one or more children at least once weekly. Louis Harris and Associates (1975) reported 55 percent of the older people had seen a child within the last day or so (including those they lived with) and 81 percent within the last week or two. While these percentages differ slightly, it is clear that older parents are frequently in contact with their children.

Hill (Aldous and Hill, 1965; Hill et al., 1970), in a uniquely controlled sample (grandparents, parents, adult children), shows generational variation in visiting patterns in one hundred Minneapolis three-generation families, biased toward the low-income level. Seventy percent of the married young adults saw their parents weekly, but only 10 percent saw their grandparents weekly. Forty percent of the middle-aged saw their parents weekly (and 70 percent saw their children). The middle-aged interact with both ascendant and descendant kin and thus visit the most, though more with their children than with their parents.

In rural Iowa, older men interacted with their children and other kin more often than did older women (Powers and Bultena, 1976). Because these investigators did not control for kin availability, it is hard to compare these findings with others that show more female linkage. Incidentally, two fifths of these men and one third of the women had no close friends outside their immediate family.

Atchley, Pignatiello, and Shaw (1975) examined differences among older women in interactions with available relatives on the basis of status and occupational type. Their findings concur with others (e.g., Schulman, 1975) that married women are less involved in kinship networks than are women of other marital status. The never-married saw their parents and siblings somewhat more frequently and the widowed the most. The same pattern holds for interaction with children for those women who had children.

In a national study of male kinship across the adult life span, Klatsky (1972) found that the age of sons did not affect patterns of contact with fathers who lived in different cities but did influence visiting frequency when fathers lived in the same city. Contact with their fathers was lowest for men under forty-five. Although they seemed higher for men between forty-five to sixty-five, further analysis showed this was due to varying probabilities of having a living father and sharing a household with him. When these factors were controlled, sons between forty-five and sixty-four whose fathers lived in the same city had the lowest rate of contact with them.

Often, visiting between older parents and their children involves no more than a brief conversation "catching up on the time of day." Sometimes, in the case of aged parents, it may be a kind of monitoring—checking to see that all is well. Often such visiting also

includes other activities: shopping, commercial and outdoor recreation, or religious activities. Those who do not live near each other
maintain contact by telephoning and letter writing; by periodically getting together for family ritual occasions such as birthdays, anniver-
saries, weddings, and funerals; by exchanging visits at holidays such as
Thanksgiving and Christmas, or during vacations. Types of contact
vary in prevalence over the life cycle. Much visiting was by telephone
even if they lived nearby.

Younger women visited with their mothers more than did older
women (perhaps more had mothers still living). A study of newlyweds
by Ryder (1968; Ryder and Goodrich, 1966) found that some have little
contact with their parents, and others visit and telephone often and still
use their parents' closet space, checking and charge accounts, car, and
so on. Those who have the closest contacts with parents are more
interested in becoming parents themselves, while those who have cut
themselves off most from their parents are more interested in "expressive sexuality" and less in having children. It would be interesting to
see if these patterns persist over the years.

The *visiting linkage,* like the residential linkage, is generally
stronger along the female line. In fact, husbands are more likely to be
in touch with their wives' parents than with their own, unless the wife
mediates contact with the husband's parents (Reiss, 1962;
Komarovsky, 1964; Leichter and Mitchell, 1967; Adams, 1971). The
order of frequency of interaction among New York Jewish families is
with wife's mother, husband's mother, wife's father and husband's
father (Leichter and Mitchell, 1967). Couples who remarry in old age
tend to visit their children along a same-sex line, according to McKain
(1969): fathers with their sons and mothers with their daughters.

Aid

Mutual aid is considered by many writers to be a critical variable in determining extended-family status. Aid may be either in the
form of services, such as babysitting, shopping, or house cleaning, or
in money or money equivalents, such as gifts. At least eleven studies
have investigated this dimension.

Bracey (1966) found that less than 15 percent of the older
people in his Louisiana sample got *regular* help (with everyday household duties) from their sons and daughters. The most frequent services
they received were shopping and housework, followed by cooking and

advisory help about financial and maintenance matters. Regular financial help from a son or daughter was received by no more than 9 percent of the older people, and an additional 4 percent said they had occasional money gifts. Atchley (1976) found even less help: about 3 percent of retired couples report cash gifts from family and friends. Bracey, however, found no evidence of real neglect of old people by their children where there was obvious need. Thus helping was specific, not generalized.

Riley and Foner (1968) state: "Contrary to the often-held theory of a one-way flow of contributions to old people, the flow of support between aged parents and their adult offspring appears to be two-directional, from parent to child or from child to parent as need and opportunity dictate. Altogether, the proportions of old people who give help to their children tends to exceed the proportions who receive help from their children" (pp. 551–552). Their conclusion is based largely upon data collected by Streib (1965), and by Shanas et al. (1968). Schorr (1960) and Hill et al. (1970) reported the same kind of aid pattern (see Table 5.1).

Hill (1965) concluded that his group of grandparents generally gave less often than they received for most categories of mutual aid. The differences in these results may stem from social class differences in the samples used. In the middle class, considerable aid continues to flow from old parents to middle-aged children even into old age, but in the working class, more help goes to old parents from middle-aged children (Schorr, 1960; Shanas et al., 1968; Adams, 1968a; Sussman and Burchinal, 1962a). A key factor in patterns of mutual aid appears to be the financial and physical capacities of older parents to offer aid.

Mutual aid patterns differ considerably by the type of aid being exchanged. Hill's (1970) findings on mutual aid patterns in one hundred three-generation families are shown in Table 5.1. We are usually quite willing to assume that the differential between help given and help received would be greatest for older people in the economic sphere, particularly since so many older people are poor. Yet the differential in the economic sphere turned out, in fact, to be the smallest. In terms of emotional gratification, household management, and illness, grandparents received much more than they gave, but in the economic area, grandparents gave almost as much as they received. The middle generation was the one that apparently gave the most in terms of economic aid. Hill's findings are less likely to be applicable to upper-middle-class families, where the oldest generation might continue to control the largest resources.

Table 5.1. Comparison of Help Received and Help Given by Generation for Chief Problem Areas[a]

	Type of Crisis			
	Economic		*Emotional Gratification*	
	Gave Percent	*Received Percent*	*Gave Percent*	*Received Percent*
Total	100	100	100	100
Grandparents	26	34	23	42
Parents	41	17	47	37
Married children	34	49	31	21

Source: Hill et al., 1970, Table 3.04, p. 67.
[a] Percents may not total 100 due to rounding.

Another important point is the extent to which aid is exchanged. The picture is very balanced in exchange of economic aid across generations. It is uneven in child care, for obvious reasons, and it varies for the other kinds of aid. No one generation comes off clearly a giver or receiver when all types of aid are considered. Three patterns of family aid may exist: a straight-line flow from old to young, an up-and-down flow from the middle generation to their parents and children, and a reciprocal flow among all generations. Sex, marital status, social class, and health variables may all intervene to produce differing results. Sex and social class effects are discussed separately later.

As a general rule, it would seem that parents continue to give to their children one way or another for as long as they are able. A shift from this pattern may therefore coincide with a deterioration in the financial or health condition of the parents. Studies that have focused on health (Shanas, 1962; Shanas et al., 1968; Rosow, 1965b) show the importance of this variable:

> In illness from a third to two-fifths rely for help with housework, meals and shopping upon husbands and wives and a similar proportion upon children or other relatives . . . Between eight and nine in every ten of the bedfast at home depend primarily on members of their families for meals, housework, personal aid, and so on. . . . (Shanas et al., pp. 428–429)

| | | Type of Crisis | | | |
| Household Management | | Child Care | | Illness | |
Gave Percent	Received Percent	Gave Percent	Received Percent	Gave Percent	Received Percent
100	100	100	100	100	100
21	52	16	0	32	61
47	23	50	23	21	21
33	25	34	78	47	18

In 1967, nearly two million persons aged fifty-five and over were receiving personal or medical care in their home; 80 percent of this care was by family members—probably children (Wilder, 1972).

Family Values

Obviously, the trends presented here are far from uniform. The different patterns in the family lives of older people could result largely from differences in *values*. Kerckhoff (1966a,b) has done one of the most thorough studies of this subject. He found three relatively clear norm-value clusters in parent/child relationships, based mainly on older people's conceptions. In what he called the *extended family* cluster, both husband and wife expected to live near their children, to enjoy considerable mutual aid and affection, and to divide the family tasks between husband and wife according to a definition of woman's work and man's work. These people did not attach much value to change, and they saw considerable conflict between self-improvement for the children and familistic values. At the other end of the continuum was the *nucleated family cluster,* in which the older couple expected neither to live near their children nor to aid or be aided by them. They expected husband and wife to share equally in household tasks, accepted change as good, and saw little conflict between family values and children's attempts to improve their social position. A third cluster, called a *modified extended family,* believed in mutual aid and affection, rejected living nearby as a necessity, and took an intermediate position on the other values. This third group was middle-of-the-roaders.

Kerckhoff found that these norm-value clusters were strongly related to social position. Families in the extended family cluster were very likely to have husbands with blue-collar occupations and low levels of education, to have lived on a farm, to have not moved around much in their lives, and to have large families. In other words, the extended family cluster was associated with a complex of characteristics we normally link with the rural working class. Those in the nucleated family cluster tended to be just the opposite—to have a husband with a white-collar occupation, to have high levels of education, to be city-reared, to have been geographically mobile, and to have relatively small families. Those in the modified extended family cluster were again in between on all measures, but tended more toward the extended family pole. About 20 percent of the families fell into the extended family cluster and 20 percent into the nucleated family cluster, with the remaining 60 percent in the modified extended family cluster.

It appears that most older people are getting about what they think they ought to have from the parent/child relationship. This is not surprising, since Troll et al. (1969) and Troll and Bengtson (1978) point to a noteworthy similarity of values across generations.

In comparing the differences between the norm-value clusters he found and actual family experiences, Kerckhoff brings up an interesting point. Since most of the couples actually show the modified extended family pattern, those who hold extended family values are likely to be disappointed in their expectations, while those who hold the nucleated family view are apt to be pleasantly surprised by more mutual aid and affection than they had expected. All of the historical changes in occupation, education, and urban/rural residence lead us to expect that the proportion identifying with the extended family cluster will decline in the future.

Quality of Relationship

While proximity, interaction frequency, and mutual aid are important indices of adult parent/child relationships, *qualitative* aspects of their relationship, such as degree of closeness or strength of feelings (affection or dislike), are perhaps even more revealing. Not until recently, however, have investigators started to explore these more intangible and covert aspects of kin relationships. There are many investigations of the quantitative aspects, but only a handful that study qualitative aspects. In our discussion, we will examine two possible qualitative indices: *intergenerational continuity* and *feelings*.

Intergenerational Continuity

Troll and Bengtson (1978), after reviewing the available literature on generations in the family, concluded that there is substantial but selective intergenerational continuity within the family. Parent/child similarity is most noticeable in religious and political affiliations, least in sex roles and personality. Social and historical forces—cohort and period effects—serve as moderator variables. Similarity is greater in areas where social forces encourage such values or behavior. It is less in areas where social forces counteract them. The evidence for a sex link in personality and value similarity is not conclusive. Some studies show that children are more like their mothers than their fathers, but other studies lead to the opposite conclusion. The sex of the child does not appear to be a relevant variable in parent/child similarity. In general, the relative influence of parents and friends appears to be of a complementary rather than an oppositional nature. Thus, people appear to choose friends who reinforce their family's values or personality styles. Furthermore, the qualitative aspects of family relationships do not seem to be significantly tied to parent/child similarity. Even when they disagree, they continue to see each other. Finally, the effect of parent's or child's age or position in their life course cannot be separated from historical effects, so far as similarities between parent and child generations are concerned.

Feelings

Many writers assume that closeness is synonymous with *liking* or *loving* and that estrangement indicates negative feelings—that we love those relatives we feel close to and hate those we feel distant from. There is evidence, however, that we cannot separate positive from negative feelings this way. Where feelings run high, they are rarely only positive or only negative (Troll and Smith, 1976; Bengtson et al., 1976; Lowenthal et al., 1975). Where love is to be found, so can hate.

Furthermore, as noted in Chapter 2, there is probably an *ebb and flow* in most family relationships.

In general, most parents and children report positive feelings for each other at all ages. It is true that we have to be cautious of self-report data, but the consistency of these reports across ages and across studies should be respected. Even high school students rarely say they do not feel close to their own parents (Kandel and Lesser, 1972; Douvan and Adelson, 1966; Bengtson, 1970). Studies of college students (Troll et al., 1969; Freeman, 1972; Bengtson and Black, 1973) show that they and their parents may think there is a generation gap in society as a whole but they rarely perceive one in their own family, and this is as true of student radicals as it is of more general samples (Angres, 1975). Most middle-aged parents in the Lowenthal et al. (1975) San Francisco sample felt good about their children. About half had only positive things to say about them, and only about 10 percent of the middle-aged and none of those in their sixties had any strong negative comments. For older ages, Bengtson and Black (1973) found high levels of regard reported by both old parents and their middle-aged children. The old parents, however, reported higher levels of sentiment while their children reported higher levels of giving help. It seems that parents remain important to their children throughout the life of the children. When adults of all ages were asked to describe a person, they tended spontaneously to refer to their parents more frequently than to any other person (Troll, 1972b). The oldest members of Troll's sample, in their seventies and eighties, were still using parents as reference persons.

In a Boston study (Johnson and Bursk, 1977), there was a significant correlation between ratings of their relationship provided by older parents and by one of their adult children. Occasionally, the parents rated their relationship higher than their child had. Both generations felt better about each other when the parents were in good health and able to be financially independent. There was also a positive correlation between the ratings and the parents' positive attitudes about aging. Whether the good feelings were engendered by absence of trouble or whether they induced better health and well-being, it is not possible to say.

Brown (1974) also found that parents over fifty-five rate their relationships with immediate family members very positively. Only 7 percent admitted that these were less than "very satisfactory." As in the findings of Adams (1968a) and Angres (1975), there appeared to be no relation between ratings and amount of contact, though this may be partly an artifact of the high level of satisfaction expressed. At any rate, only 30 percent said they saw their children less frequently in 1971 than they had in 1961.

Cumming and Henry (1961), with a Kansas City sample of people over age fifty, were also interested in the quality of family relationships. Respondents were asked whom they felt closest to; in most cases, it was to their child or children. They felt almost as close to their parents as well, if they were alive. This parental or filial attachment (with *ascendant/descendant* rather than *collateral* kin) was stronger than that toward siblings and spouse, but it did not extend to grandchildren, where the feelings reported were much weaker. (Grandparenting is discussed in Chapter 6.) Rosow (1967), with a Cleveland sample of people over sixty-five, was interested in *emotional dependence* on children and its relation to contacts with neighbors. He found (1) wide individual differences in emotional dependence, and (2) no relation between this attitude and other behavior, such as contacts with neighbors. Neighbors did not usually substitute for children.

Unfortunately, much of the research in this area suffers from having to rely on reports by only one side of a dyad or family. We do not know how the children of respondents interviewed by Brown or by Cumming and Henry felt about their parents, nor whether parents of Adams's (1968a) young adult respondents reciprocated their feelings of intimacy and "positive concern." What we *can* say is that older parents do not tend to disengage from their children, regardless of their expressed satisfaction (Brown, 1974; Ingraham, 1974). As stated in Chapter 2, disengagement in old age seems to be *into* rather than *from* the family. Furthermore, Cumming and Henry (1961) found that while friends can often substitute for lost siblings, they rarely substitute for missing children. They explain this in terms of *emotional dependence,* as does Rosow (1967).

Duty

As cited in Chapter 2, not all relations between parents and their children are characterized by affection and emotional ties. Many times, feelings of *obligation* or a sense of duty underlie frequent visiting and aid. Alternatively, it may be either shame that others would consider one delinquent in expected duties or a more internalized guilt. For example, Lozier and Althouse (1974) found that in one Appalachian community, children were heavily involved with their parents because they knew that negative community opinion would follow from failure to meet their obligations.

Kohlberg (1973) sees the higher states of moral development resulting from having had to make irrevocable moral decisions or choices. It is possible that the point at which adult children achieve filial maturity is the point at which they must assume responsibility for some aspects of their parents' lives and live with the results of acting on decisions growing out of those responsibilities. In helping parents, children often learn more about them. It is much easier to assume that you "know" someone when you do not have to create conditions that will fit their attitudes and preferences. At the same time, many older parents can get to know their children better.

Blenkner (1965) believed that *filial maturity* occurs in middle age. It is at this point that we first see our parents as real people. Erikson (1959) also speaks of middle age as the time of changing perspective in feelings toward our parents, when we can first truly appreciate them and see the relevance of their lives for ours. So far, there is little research evidence for this assumption.

Adams (1967b, 1968b), who compared friendship and kinship ties in terms of Parsons's interaction theory, postulated that relations between kin are dominated by intimacy and *positive concern,* which lead to feelings of obligation or duty and which tend to persist over time, spatial separation, and occupational mobility. Relations with friends, on the other hand, are characterized by *value consensus,* and while they may be more desired at the moment, they less often persist over time and mobility. He compares the interactions reported by his North Carolina respondents with their best friends, parents, nearest-age sibs, and best-known cousins, and found relations with parents the closest and most obligatory and relations with friends the highest in value consensus. Sibs were in the middle. Pending further research into qualitative differences in relationships both in and out of the family, we can only speculate about the significance of a parent/child attachment that may persist throughout life and be transferred to the next generation of parents and children, but not to more peripheral relationships—even sibs, and even grandchildren.

Adams (1968a) found that when parents lived nearby, affectional closeness had little effect upon interaction frequency. Neither affection nor agreement on values influenced visiting frequency. Among "close" sons, one third saw their parents often; among "distant" sons, one third saw their parents often. Yet the *reasons* for keeping in touch varied by the degree of affectional closeness to either or both parents. Obligation or a combination of obligation and enjoyment were much more frequent answers by children who said they did not feel close to either parent. Children who felt close to one or both parents were more likely to say they visited because of enjoyment or a combination of enjoyment and obligation.

The obligatory motive in interaction between aged parents and their adult children is commonly assumed. For example, Schorr (1960) speaks of filial obligation or responsibility and at one point equates the adult-offspring/older-parent situation with the parent/young child situation, both in a balance is necessary in family obligations and aid. Where point that a balance is necessary in family obligations and aid. Where the mother is a widow, the mother/daughter relationship is smoother and closer than the mother/son relationship, because mothers and daughters can reciprocate services but mothers and sons cannot. Consequently, mutual enjoyment and affection between mothers and sons tend to decrease following the mother's widowhood. Adams found that when a parent was widowed, the greatest interaction and aid exchange was between daughters and widowed mothers in a reciprocal pattern. Sons said they kept in touch with a widowed parent because they felt obligation, daughters because they enjoyed it. Both sons and daughters said, however, that they felt less close than before their parent's widowhood. Can it be that an increased feeling of obligation acts to diminish closeness? Middle-aged mothers admit that they feel differently about their sons and daughters. They expect more interaction and help from their daughters and are upset when they don't get it. They expect much less from their sons and are delighted with anything they get (Hagestad, 1977).

Overview of Quality of Relationships

Clark and Anderson (1967) state:

> A good relationship with children in old age depends, to large extent, on the graces and autonomy of the aged parent—in short, on his ability to manage gracefully by himself. It would appear that, in our culture, there simply cannot be any happy role reversals between the generations, neither an increasing dependency of parent upon child not a continuing reliance of child upon parent. The mores do not sanction it and children and parents resent it. The parent must remain strong and independent. If his personal resources fail, the conflicts arise. The child, on the other hand, must not threaten the security of

> the parent with request for monetary aid or other care when parental income has shrunk through retirement. *The ideal situation is when both parent and child are functioning well.* [Italics ours] The parent does not depend on the child for nurturance or social interaction; these needs the parent can manage to fulfill by himself elsewhere. He does not limit the freedom of his child nor arouse the child's feelings of guilt. The child establishes an independent dwelling, sustains his own family, and achieves a measure of the hope the parent had entertained for him. Such an ideal situation, of course, is more likely to occur when the parent is still provided with a spouse and where a high socioeconomic status buttresses the parent and child (pp. 275–276).

Their conclusion is consistent with most research findings. For example, Johnson and Bursk (1977) found that health and finances were major factors in family relations. Older parents who are in poor health tend to be less satisfied with their lives, and this dissatisfaction tends to color their relationships with their children. In addition, fear of financial difficulties might cause family friction. Poor health and poverty contribute to dependency, and the greater the dependency, the more likely parents and children are to have negative feelings toward themselves and toward each other. One reason for older people's fear of dependency may relate to value differences between generations. Differences in lifestyle, childrearing attitudes, and religious practices may make daily dependent contact difficult. This is particularly hard when the older generation is foreign-born and there may thus be extreme differences in beliefs and practices.

Given the difficulties of dependency, we might expect in general to find a great deal of alienation between very old parents and their children. This notion is particularly prevalent among people who work with disabled older people and their families. Nevertheless, study after study has failed to find any general alienation. As Blenkner (1965, p. 48) says:

> the older person prefers to maintain his independence as long as he can, but . . . when he can no longer manage for himself, he expects his children to assume that responsibility; his children in turn expect to, and do, undertake it, particularly in terms of personal and protective services.

Sussman and Burchinal (1962a) found that illness of an older parent usually brought an almost instantaneous response from children. In fact, close ties with children were particularly prevalent among the very old. Shanas and her associates (1968) found that among older people with children, 98 percent of women and 72 percent of men who were *over eighty* either lived with a child or within ten minutes of one.

Perhaps the reasons for the alienation myth are to be found in the attitudes of professionals who work with older people. These people are perhaps in the worst position to judge. Their view of the situation is biased by the fact that, by definition, the older people they see are disproportionately alienated and neglected; otherwise, there would be no occasion for them to seek professional help (Blenkner, 1965).

The evidence indicates that most parents understand and comply with the norms for older-parent/adult-child relationships. These norms specify that older parents recognize the right of their adult children to lead their own lives. Many parents believe that if they are too demanding, they will alienate their children. At the same time, the adult children are expected to leave behind the emancipation-oriented behavior of early adulthood and to turn again to their parents "no longer as a child, but as a mature adult with a new role and a different love, seeing him for the first time as an individual with his own rights, needs, limitations, and a life history that, to a large extent, made him the person he is long before his child existed" (Blenkner, 1965, p. 58).

In conclusion, then, the theme of most current research findings is that what older parents really want is continued contact with their children along with continued independence. Most really need little help, except in times of illness, and when they need it, it is usually provided. They continue to want to help their children, not only financially when they have the resources, but also with occasional babysitting, other services, or gifts. They generally do not feel the need to rely upon their children for social companionship. Perhaps their greatest need continues to be for respect and dignity. There is no evidence that their children neglect them.

Sex Differences

As suggested earlier, adult-child/older-parent relationships may be influenced by whether the relationship is mother/daughter, mother/son, father/daughter, or father/son. The literature is fairly consistent about the solidarity among women in the family; mother/daughter ties tend to be stronger than mother/son ties from adulthood on. Among the second-generation Italians in Boston studied by Gans (1962), the mother/married daughter tie is the only viable cross-generational one, since with this exception, kinship interaction tends to be confined to relatives of the same sex *and* same generation.

Turner (1975) suggests that because of our social norms, emancipation problems are difficult but necessary for men. He claims that not only must sons break their ties with their parents at adulthood, but when they marry they have to shift even further toward autonomy. Daughters are encouraged to continue their relations with their mothers and they often carry over a dependent orientation into marriage. This sex-differential training with respect to independence may create lasting differences in ties to the family of orientation.

Lowenthal and her associates (1975), in their cross-sectional study of four life stages, report that both men and women—in every age group—said they felt closer to their mothers almost twice as often as they said they felt close to their fathers. On the other hand, older women experienced more satisfying relationships with their daughters, and older men preferred their oldest sons.

While most of the studies report a bias toward female-linked kinship networks, with residence closer to wife's parents, interaction greater with wife's relatives, mutual aid more frequent along the female line, and affection greater among the women, Adams (1968a) found relatively little sex differentiation in kinship interrelations except for patterns of mutual aid. Greensboro women shopped with their mothers and received more patterned aid (babysitting and gifts) from their parents than men did from their parents. On the other hand, more men than women *gave* help in both money and services (work in the house) to their parents, and joined them in out-of-the-home recreation. Similarly, Albrecht (1962) found no preference for sharing rituals with the mother's side of the family over the father's side in a middle-class sample of 252 extended families, one third of which included people over age seventy.

Robins and Tomanec (1962) also found no sex difference among young adults in closeness to family (parents and sibs). And although others have stated that females are the kin keepers, Wake and Sporakowski (1972) found that the women they interviewed were somewhat less willing to support aged parents than men. When they controlled for generation, however, this sex difference disappeared.

Another possible mode of sex differences in family relationships is sex lineages: a male line of grandfather/father/son as distinguished from a female line of grandmother/mother/daughter. Aldous and Hill (1965) reported sex differences in transmission of role behavior over three generations. Male lineages showed greater continuity in religion and occupation than in other traits; female lineages were even more alike in religion than the male, but not in occupation. This study, however, antedated the women's movement and the influx of women into the labor market.

One of the rare longitudinal studies of parents was started at Berkeley in 1928 and most recently followed up by Maas and Kuypers (1974) in the late 1960s, when the parents were between sixty and eighty-two. There seem to be several types of fathers. The most common type was family centered (40 percent); these fathers had a close relationship with their wives and children, and some even with their siblings. Another 23 percent of the fathers were satisfied with the level of affection for and from the children, but had little face-to-face interaction with them. About 36 percent of the fathers had low levels of both affection and interaction with their children.

There was a greater variety of parent/child relationships among the mothers. To begin with, and contrary to other findings, only about 21 percent had very high satisfaction and involvement with their adult children. About 65 percent had relatively low involvement with their children (compared to other involvements), and 13 percent of the older mothers even had a strained parent/child relationship.

A final note on sex differences is provided by Adams's (1968a) finding that even though women may not agree with their parents' values, they still feel close to them and visit them often. This is less true for men. Adams also found a curious sex difference in feelings about parents. Daughters' affections for their fathers were related to their fathers' occupational position. They appreciated their fathers more if the fathers had higher status. Sons, on the other hand, related to their mothers in terms of their own status. The more successful the son, the more he appreciated his mother.

Social Class Differences

On the whole, *social class differences* in kin relations are not as large as sex differences. Kin relations, however, tend to be more sex segregated among working-class families (see the observations of Garigue, 1962 on French Canadians and of Gans, 1962 on Boston Italians). Father/son and mother/daughter ties are more commonly reported for working-class samples (Aldous, 1967; McKain, 1969) and run counter to the more general rule of female sex linkage.

Social class differences may also explain the contradictory findings about help patterns across generations reported above. In middle-class samples (Schorr, 1960 and Shanas et al., 1968), considerable help continues to flow from old parents to middle-aged children into old age, while among blue-collar families, more help goes from middle-aged children to old parents. Working-class parents give services, middle-class parents give financial aid (Adams, 1968a; Hill et al., 1970; Sussman and Burchinal, 1962a). Since the giving of services is restricted to children or parents who live nearby but financial help is not so geographically limited, middle-class families are not as affected by geographic mobility as are working-class families. Thus, Litwak's (1960a,b) proposition that the modified extended family continues family aid in the face of geographic mobility may be more appropriate for middle-class than working-class populations. Adams does suggest, however, that since it is usually easier for working-class people to find a job nearby, they are not likely to move far from kin unless they are already estranged. Middle-class families sometimes find it necessary to move about for purposes of establishing careers, no matter how they might feel about leaving their relatives, even if they tend to return close to them again later.

It may be that help is greatest at the extremes of economic situations. The poor need and seek help from their relatives, and the rich get it and give in gifts and inheritance. Aldous (1965) suggested that this could have opposite effects on nuclear family integration; the conjugal solidarity of the poor husband and wife may be weakened by needing outside help, but the upper-class family would press for survival of a marriage for dynastic reasons and insure it with financial inducements.

This suggestion of a curvilinear relationship between social status and aid is disputed by Wake and Sporakowski (1972) who found no differences in attitudes about filial responsibility between lower-, middle-, and upper-class people. When social status was held constant, however, more members of the younger generation than of the older believed that parents should be taken care of or supported by their children. Whether this difference is due to age/role position in the life cycle (youthful idealism versus adult realism) or to cohort differences remains to be examined.

Geographic and Social Mobility

The great virtue of an isolated nuclear family would be its freedom to move, both upward and outward, in response to the demands of an industrialized, bureaucratized society. This can be found more among middle-class families, who move more and live farther apart in miles. Yet in terms of absolute interaction frequency or of presumed strength of ties, they show little difference from working-class patterns, and that limited difference is in the direction of even greater visiting among the middle class.

There have been a number of interesting studies of migration effects on kinship (Berardo, 1967a,b; Booth and Camp, 1974; Bultena 1969a; Bultena and Marshall, 1970; Jitodai, 1963; Rieger, 1972; Schwarzweller, 1964; Schwarzweller and Seggar, 1967). When these findings are pooled, one cannot escape a mounting conviction that disruptive effects on kinship ties are at most only temporary. As Litwak (1960b) suggests, kin ties in the modified extended family may even assist a nuclear unit's geographic venture for occupational advancement. Furthermore, Britton and Britton (1967) found that older people in a rural area in Pennsylvania, while they missed their distant children, reported increased morale and pride at their success. Among most Americans, achievement values override familism values. There is a tendency after a period of time for some older parents, past retirement, to move near their now-settled middle-aged children—that is, if these middle-aged children have not already moved back near their parents. Eventually, more kin may be available to those who have moved to the new area than to those who stayed behind.

Miller's (1972) research provided empirical evidence that economic aspirations were a more important factor than extended family orientations in predicting propensity to migrate. This was generally true for both husbands and wives, and for people both with and without parents and siblings residing in the same community. This relationship, however, is highly influenced by the nuclear family life cycle (Miller, 1976). Among couples who have parents and/or siblings living in the same community, migration intentions are inversely related to attitudinal orientation toward their extended family (Miller, 1973). Although strong positive extended family orientations may operate for many as a deterrent to migration, there is typically no long-term detrimental impact on extended family relations for those who do migrate. This is consistent with other research that finds no difference between migrants and nonmigrants in solidarity with their parents (Rieger, 1972).

Social mobility is not generally related to breaking up of the extended family, but some special effects of downward mobility should be mentioned. Parent/child visiting patterns are not affected by downward mobility of the child, but siblings and more distant kin do tend to become estranged as a result, so that there is a general disintegrating effect (Adams, 1967b; Aldous, 1967). Rosenberg (1970) and Pope

(1964) note that in the long run, the effect of a financial crisis such as a prolonged period of unemployment is less frequent contact between that individual and his relatives, even though at first kin visiting is increased (presumably to help with the crisis).

Adult-Child/Older-Parent Relations over the Life Course

Studies of older-parent/adult-child relations have looked mainly at the launching stage, when parents are in early middle age, and at aged parents and their middle-aged children. Furthermore, wide age and developmental ranges tend to be collapsed into single categories. There is no research on two categories of parents and children: those where the children are in their thirties and early forties and those where the children are themselves past middle age. Findings have been reported on the close links between newly married couples and their parents. On one hand is the American norm that requires independence of the newly married couple. They are expected to establish a home separate from both sets of parents (*neolocal*), raise their children according to "absolute" criteria for "correct" childrearing and not listen to the "old-fashioned wisdom" of their grandparents (whom most psychotherapists see chiefly as malevolent influences on nuclear family integration and childrearing success), and be economically independent by virtue of the young husband's own efforts and successes. In actual fact, most young couples seem to live reasonably close to both sets of parents, receive either help in the form of services (such as babysitting) or money (more in the middle class), and visit frequently.

At the other end of the age scale is an opposite stereotype. The old parent is believed to want dependence on his adult children, to demand money and services, and to move in with children where possible, though generally to be neglected and unwanted. Again, the facts are just the opposite. Most old parents prefer to live alone, though they live near and see their children frequently and there seems to be as much reciprocity as dependence in services and money, with aged parents continuing to help their children as long as they can.

What happens in the years between? Are the bonds between the nuclear units continued throughout? Or do they loosen gradually and only tighten again as the parents retire? Does the involvement of adult children in rearing their own children loosen ties with their parents? How influential is the adult child's career upon potential changes in ties with parents over the life course? The cross-sectional and longitudinal data we need to answer such questions are practically nonexistent.

The small sample of parents, studied by Lowenthal and associates (1975), who were middle-aged or approaching retirement

> . . . looked back to the time when their children were infants as the period of greatest parental happiness. In so doing, they may in part be indulging in pleasant recollections of their more youthful selves, or reflecting more contemporary experiences of carefree interaction with grandchildren. For the most part, they were nostalgic for a period free of parent-child conflict, a period when, whatever the stresses, the child's dependence on the parents is unquestioned and his expressions of love more frequent and direct. . . . for older men the next most satisfying relationships occurred after the children had fully matured. (Lowenthal et al., 1975, p. 40)

Some of the consequences of Blenkner's (1965, 1969) concept of *filial maturity* discussed earlier are important for a life-cycle theory of development. A basic corollary is the reciprocity of the developmental process. For the child to achieve filial maturity, the parent must participate in the process, first in a modeling capacity, and second in a rewarding capacity. There is reason to believe that the inverse is also true. For the parent to continue to develop, the child must participate in the process in both a modeling and a rewarding capacity. In other words, the significance of the parent/child relationship does not end with launching but continues throughout life. Parents and children who continue to develop throughout their lives—to accept their own development as meaningful and satisfying—are helping their children and parents to develop in turn. The question of reciprocity and balance in parent/child relationships has been touched on earlier.

Sources of Change

There are several sources of change in adult-child/older-parent relationships. We will discuss retirement, widowhood, and divorce or separation.

As mentioned earlier, retirement can give older parents freedom to move nearer to their children. But retirement, with its average income decline of 50 percent, can also make traveling to visit adult children more difficult. For the most part, loss of job through retirement is not a source of declining prestige within the family. Those persons who own family businesses, however, can lose a good bit of power and influence upon retirement. For example, farmers who operate two- or three-generation family farms tend to lose their power over economic decision making when they hand their farms down to their children. Consequently, many older farmers don't completely retire. They give up physical work, but continue to manage the farm.

Widowhood generally increases interaction with children during the bereavement period, but it has little long-run effect except for those widowed persons who move in with adult children or whose adult children move in with them. As we saw earlier, this is not a common pattern.

We do not know how divorce or separation affects adult-child/older-parent relationships. There are a good many ideas that could be studied. Do the children of divorced parents keep in touch with both parents? Is the frequency of contact affected by divorce? Are divorced parents as likely as widowed parents to receive aid from their children? Do older divorced mothers become financially dependent on their children more frequently than widows do? What effect does the timing of the divorce in the adult child's life have on the effect of divorce on parent/child relations? Does divorce affect parent/child relationships for mothers more than for fathers? The list of questions that need study is long.

Summary

Most older Americans have living children, and those who do are in close touch with them. They do not tend to live in the same household unless either parents or children are in such poor health that they cannot take care of themselves or unless financial circumstances make it necessary. That is, all prefer to be as autonomous and independent as they are able, and are happier when they can be so. When help is needed, however, it is available, most often from parent or child, much less frequently from more distant relatives. Parents and their adult children seem to prefer to live near each other, as witnessed by both prevalence and migration data. When they move apart for economic or career reasons, they tend to move closer together again later in life. How much of this enduring relationship is intrinsic strength of bonds, meaningfulness and enjoyment of each other's company, and how much is instrumental duty or obligation motivated by shame or guilt, we cannot say. It is not impossible, however, that all kinds of motives underlie such long-standing and complex relationships. Most ties are strongest between women—mothers and daughters—though ethnic and social class factors may mediate this tendency. Social class may be an important mediating factor in flow of help, with the oldest generation continuing to supply most help—particularly money—in middle and upper classes and the middle generation supplying to both older and younger generations in working and lower classes. Over time, family crises may lead to short-term increase or mobilization of interaction and help. Nevertheless, downward mobility of one member may eventuate in reduced interaction and help in the long run.

Chapter Six

Being a Grandparent or Great-Grandparent

The role of grandparent may be seen from two perspectives: that of the person occupying the role or that of the grandchildren. The chief emphasis in this book is upon the grandparents themselves.

Unfortunately, most of the literature on grandparents tends to neglect grandfathers. It has been suggested (Nye and Berardo, 1973b) that men postpone intense involvement in the grandfather role until after retirement. This hypothesis is as yet unverified. It may also be that there tend to be more grandmothers around than grandfathers, since women tend to live longer and bear children earlier.

Prevalence

Grandparenting has become a phenomenon of middle age rather than old age. Earlier marriage, earlier childbirth, and longer life expectancy are producing grandparents in their forties. These grandparents, because they themselves have only a few children, are truly grandparents in identity, and not at the same time parents of young children. The increase of families with three and four generations has made grandparenting a second- rather than a first-generation (not the oldest generation, in other words) event. In addition, grandmothers as well as grandfathers now tend to be employed. This change from the earlier rocking-chair image of grandparents could have far-reaching consequences in adult socialization and role modeling, as well as in family interaction. Furthermore, as Shanas et al. (1968) point out, a woman of fifty or sixty can be caring for an elderly mother of seventy or eighty, and thus divided in her loyalty among the different generations in her family.

About three fourths of the older people in the United States have living grandchildren. Among grandparents, about the same proportion see their grandchildren at least every week or two. Nearly half of all American grandparents see a grandchild every day or so (Harris and Associates, 1975). Few grandparents live in the same household with a grandchild, however; only about 5 percent of the households headed by older people contain grandchildren (Atchley, 1977), and as noted in earlier chapters, it is rare for grandparents and grandchildren to live in households headed by an adult child who would be a parent to the grandchildren.

In the 1970 census, the proportion of older people living with an adult child increased with age. Up to 20 percent of seventy-five to seventy-nine year olds did so. Still, among all those older people who were living with an adult child, over half—55 percent of these households, regardless of who was the household head—had no children under eighteen present.

Perceptions by Grandchildren

Several researchers (Robertson, 1976; Kahana and Kahana, 1970; Bekker and Taylor, 1966) have explored younger people's perceptions of old people in terms of the number of generations in the subject's own family. In general, young people who have grandparents and great-grandparents tend to have less age "prejudice" than those who do not, although preteenage children may show somewhat more distance from their grandparents than younger children do (Kahana and Kahana, 1970). More research is needed on attitudes toward grandparents and other old members of the family, and their impact upon children.

The value of grandparenting for young children has been demonstrated outside the family situation in foster grandparent programs with institutionalized children. The employment of poverty-level retirees, both men and women, as surrogate grandparents to emotionally deprived children has been shown to alleviate some of the symptoms traditionally associated with such deprivation, such as depression, depressed intellectual functioning, and social immaturity (Saltz, 1970).

Table 6.1.   Intergenerational Visiting According to Gender[a]

	Parent/Grandparents		Child/Parents	
(percent)	*Male*	*Female*	*Male*	*Female*
Daily	6	15	32	21
Weekly	30	39	42	48
Monthly	52	39	23	25
Quarter yearly	9	6	—	6
Yearly	3	—	3	—
Number of cases	33	46	31	48

Source: Hill et al., 1970.
[a]The percentage totals do not always add to 100 because of rounding.

Several investigations have focused on the adult grandchild's feelings toward grandparents. Their results do not agree. Robins and Tomanec (1962) questioned 140 informants (mostly college students) about their attitudes toward kin: the number of avenues used for interaction, the performance of services, and the fulfillment of obligations. In this sample, grandparents were reportedly felt to be closer than aunts, uncles, and cousins, and thus next to parents and siblings. On the other hand, Adams's (1968a) Greensboro respondents reported that they interacted with aunts and uncles more frequently than with grandparents and cousins. This was 28 percent of the sample. Only 10 percent of the adults in Greensboro interacted with a grandparent more than with other secondary kin (like cousins and aunts). Adams, however, did not control for availability. While the question of rank order of importance of relatives may not be of major significance, the connection between attitudes toward relatives and other components of family organization should be worth further study.

Interaction

In Hill's (1970) major study of three-generation families of adults, interaction among all three generations was significant and continuous, although the investigators described the grandparent/

(percent)		
	Child/Grandparents	
	Male	Female
Daily	6	6
Weekly	26	35
Monthly	16	15
Quarter yearly	36	33
Yearly	16	10
Number of cases	31	48

grandchild relationship as connected through the intervening generation. The middle generation thus served as a *lineage bridge*, with the
women in that generation more prominent in this function than their
husbands. The authors comment, "To function in three generation
depth the modified extended family network would seem to require an
active 'kinkeeping' middle generation" (p. 62), The intergenerational
visiting patterns are shown in Table 6.1. Half of the grandchildren
visited their grandparents at least monthly, with the women showing a
slight edge, but not a large one (56 percent versus 50 percent). The fact
that these families all resided in the Minneapolis geographic area is, of
course, important. We should also note that these young couples visited less with their grandparents than with their parents.

Just as the parent/child relationships are affected by the respec-
tive *generational stakes* hypothesized by Bengtson and Kuypers (1971)
and discussed in Chapter 2, so may be the grandparent/grandchild relationships. Since the future would be even more foreshortened for
grandparents than for the middle generation, it may be that their wish
for continuity through their second-order (and third-order) descendants
is even greater than that of middle-aged parents. They would thus tend
to exaggerate the closeness of their ties to their grandchildren. Some
writers suggest that the difference in power relationships between
grandparents and their grandchildren as compared with parents and
children may operate to make these two generations seem more like
allies against the power of the middle generation (cf. Apple, 1956).

Apple cites cross-cultural data of grandparents who are removed from family authority and tend to have equalitarian or indulgent, warm relationships with their grandchildren. When grandparents retain economic power and prestige, their relationships with grandchildren are more authoritarian and formal. Most modern urban middle-class grandparents tend to be in the former position and enjoy their grandchildren without feeling responsible for them.

Kahana and Kahana (1970), in a small-sample study, report that maternal grandmothers and paternal grandfathers show closeness and warmth toward their grandchildren, view them as if they were their own children, and approve of their upbringing. In contrast, maternal grandfathers and paternal grandmothers express negative attitudes. These feelings are independent of the amount of interaction with their families and may reflect closer ties or more identification with same-sexed kin and the children of same-sexed kin. The age of the grandchildren in this study also affected the relationships and attitudes toward their grandparents. Children of different ages emphasized different aspects of the relationship.

Robertson (1976) studied eighty-six young adult grandchildren, ages eighteen to twenty-six. She found nearly all had positive attitudes toward grandparents and expected little from them except emotional gratification. More than half said they enjoyed being with them and felt they would help them if necessary. These data correspond closely with those of Hill et al. (1970).

As Hill et al. emphasized, parents serve as mediators or lineage bridges in this relationship. They may transfer their attitudes and behaviors toward their parents to their children, thus either facilitating or hindering interactions and the development of bonds between grandchildren and grandparents (Robertson, 1975). On the same topic, Gilford and Black (1972) found that geographic separation, which is not an important variable in the adult relationship between parents and children who had once lived together, *is* important in grandparent/grandchild relationships. The effect of separation is not simple, however. Grandparents' feelings toward their grandchildren have a direct effect on the feelings of the grandchildren with whom they can and do interact frequently—who live nearby. But when they live far apart, their relationship is contingent upon the intervening parent/child dyadic bonds. In other words, where grandparents have close ties with their children, regardless of geographic separation, they are likely to be important to their grandchildren even if they do not see each other often. As Neugarten and Weinstein (1964) said, grandparenting is an earned, not an ascribed, status. (These findings resemble those on fathers' relationships with children reported by Feldman, 1977.)

Hays and Mindel (1973) compared black and white young-adult parents on kin contact. They found greater contact with grandparents, siblings, cousins, aunts, and uncles among the black respondents then among the white. Thus, black extended kin networks may be stronger than white. Unfortunately, as noted earlier, most studies on black/white differences do not control for social class.

Grandparents' Perceptions

What are the attitudes of grandparents toward their role and toward their grandchildren? Some researchers find that the grandparent role is peripheral for many older people; it is not a central source of identity, interaction, or satisfaction to them. On the other hand, other researchers find that grandparents are in frequent contact with their grandchildren and derive great satisfaction from them.

The old people in Kansas City studied by Cumming and Henry (1961) did not feel close to their grandchildren. They were "glad to see them come and glad to see them go." Clark (1969), in San Francisco, found that grandparents liked small children more as they (the grandparents) got older because older grandchildren don't want to bother with them. Boyd (1969b) found age, sex, and class differences in the evaluation of the grandparent role. She studied forty-five upper- and middle-class and twenty-five working-class four-generation families. As found by Gilford and Black (1972) later, a stronger tie with grandparents existed when they lived nearby, particularly for the upper and middle classes.

Relationship

Atchley (1977) has suggested that grandmothers appear to have a somewhat better chance of developing a relationship with their granddaughters than grandfathers have in developing one with their grandsons. The key to this trend is the relative stability over generations of the housewife role in comparison with the occupational roles of men. It is simply a matter of the grandmothers' having more to offer their granddaughters that is pertinent to the lives they will lead. Sewing, cooking, and childrearing are but a few of the subjects that granddaughters may want to learn about. In contrast, the grandfathers very often find their skills unwanted, not only by industry but by their grandsons as well. This may be more typical of middle-class grandfathers, unless they are involved in home skills or gardening, or in sports that their grandsons could identify with. If women's roles in society change substantially, however, there is a good chance that traditional grandmothers' knowledge will also become less pertinent to the aspirations of their granddaughters. For instance, Updegraff (1968) found several areas of change in the grandmother's role when she compared three cohorts of grandmothers.

Less than half of the grandparents in Wood and Robertson's study (1976) had told their grandchildren about family history or customs, or had taught them a special skill such as cooking, sewing, fishing, or a craft. A breakdown by sex of the grandparents was not provided, however; so Atchley's hypothesis remains untested.

On the whole, the *valued grandparent* is an earned and acquired status, involving personal qualities and not automatically ascribed to the person in the position. It is like an extended parental role, and an active one. As a consequence, grandmothers, who are more experienced in the details of childrearing, may be more valued than grandfathers, provided they serve as helpers rather than substitutes. Some young mothers, particularly those who have not come to terms with their rivalry with their mothers, may try to cut down the autonomy of the grandmother. The instrumental father role can't be shared, however, so grandfathers have to become equivalent in function to grandmothers. Most studies suggest that the importance of grandparents to grandchildren is mediated by the grandparents' relationship with their children. The parents usually decide how much interaction and how much value to place upon the grandparents.

An interesting but unanswered question concerns whether grandparenting is more important or satisfying to widows than to those who have a spouse. Adams (1968b) fond that widows more often than married mothers had patterns of mutual assistance with their daughters. It would not be surprising to learn that this increased involvement also brought increased saliency to their grandparent role.

There are two major studies of the meaning of the grandparent role to the person occupying that position. These were done by Neugarten and Weinstein (1964), and by Wood and Robertson (1976) and Robertson (1977). A theoretical framework has also been provided by Kahana and Kahana (1971).

Noting that sociologists had tended to neglect grandparenthood as an aspect of the family life of older people, Neugarten and

Weinstein (1964) sought to examine three dimensions of grandparent-hood: the degree of comfort with the role, the significance of the role, and the style with which the role was enacted.

Through open-ended interviews with seventy sets of middle-class grandparents in the metropolitan Chicago area, Neugarten and Weinstein were able to secure data on how often and on what occasions the grandparents saw their grandchildren, and on the significance of grandparenthood in their lives and how it had affected them. Table 6.2 shows their results.

Table 6.2. Ease of Role Performance, Significance of Role, and Style of Grandparenting in Seventy Pairs of Grandparents

	Grand-mothers	*Grand-fathers*
	N = 70	*N = 70*
	(percent)	*(percent)*
Ease of role performance		
Comfortable/pleasant	59	61
Difficulty/discomfort	36	29
(Insufficient data)	5	10
Significance of the grandparent role		
Biological renewal and/or continuity	42[a]	23[a]
Emotional self-fulfillment	19	27
Resource person to child	4	11
Vicarious achievement through child	4	4
Remote; little effect on the self	27	29
(Insufficient data)	4	6
Style of grandparenting		
Formal	31	33
Fun-seeking	29	24
Parent surrogate	14[a]	0[a]
Reservoir of family wisdom	1	6
Distant figure	19	29
(Insufficient data)	6	8

Source: Adapted from B. Neugarten and K. Weinstein, "The Changing American Grandparent," *Journal of Marriage and the Family*. Copyright 1964 by the National Council on Family Relations. Used by permission.
[a]The difference between grandmothers and grandfathers in this category is reliable at or beyond the .05 level (frequencies were tested for differences of proportions, using the Yates correction for continuity).

While a clear majority of the grandparents expressed comfort and pleasure in the role, nearly a third were uncomfortable enough to mention this discomfort to the interviewer. The sources of discomfort or disappointment included the strain associated with thinking of oneself as a grandparent, conflict with parents over the rearing of a grandchild, and self-chastisement about indifference toward taking care of or assuming responsibility for a grandchild.

Although grandparenthood usually had multiple significance for grandparents, Neugarten and Weinstein categorized all of their respondents into one of five somewhat overlapping categories on the basis of their rating of the *primary* significance of the role. As Table 6.2 shows, the prime significance of grandparenthood was reported to be biological renewal and/or continuity: seeing oneself extended into the future. The authors of this book caution that the difference found between grandfathers and grandmothers may be because only one third were grandfathers. It is likely that men may be more inclined to trace biological continuity through sons than through daughters. It would have been interesting to hold sex of immediate offspring constant in this study, and also to examine the possibility of variation in meaningfulness among different grandchildren. For some, grandparenthood offers an opportunity to succeed in a new emotional role—to be a better grandparent than she or he was a parent.

Others in the study felt relatively remote from their grandchildren and acknowledged that grandparenthood had relatively little effect on their own lives. Most people in this category felt that theirs was an unusual sentiment, and while a few expected that as their grandchildren grew older the relationship might develop more fully, most of them—men and women alike—perceived the role of grandparent as basically meaningless.

As for *style* of grandparenting, Neugarten and Weinstein found that few of their respondents served primarily as reservoirs of family wisdom, which, considering the rapidly changing nature of knowledge, should not be surprising. Being a *parent surrogate* was apparently a style reserved for women, although few grandmothers actually performed this function. The style of the majority of grandparents was either *formal* or *distant*. The formal style emphasizes the "proper" role of a grandparent. It leaves parental functions up to the parents, although there is constant interest in the grandchildren. The distant style is similar except that contact is fleeting and infrequent—often reserved for holidays and special occasions such as Christmas or birthdays.

The *fun-seeking* style emphasizes informality and playfulness. Authority lines are considered irrelevant, and the emphasis is on making the relationship between grandparent and grandchild a mutually satisfying one. A quarter of the grandparents showed this style. Note that this is also the style described by Apple (1956).

Neugarten and Weinstein were also interested in the effect of age on the style of grandparenting. Table 6.3 shows that grandparents were most likely to be under sixty-five, and that those who were under sixty-five were much more likely to adopt a fun-seeking or distant style; whereas better than half of those over sixty-five had adopted a formal style. The authors conclude that this could be either the result of socialization processes in different eras (cohort or period effects) or simply the influence of age itself. Neugarten and Weinstein concluded that grandparenthood as a role is perhaps more salient in middle age than in later maturity or old age, particularly in terms of assumption of new roles. Perhaps more important, they also concluded that the younger grandparents are much less concerned with a style that revolves around an authority relationship than are their older counterparts.

Wood and Robertson (1976) developed a typology of four meanings of the grandparent role based on interviews with one hundred twenty-five grandmothers and one hundred thirty-two grandfathers from a stable working-class area in Madison, Wisconsin. Table 6.4 shows the four types and their distribution. Grandparents who derived a great deal of meaning from both social norms and personal experience were called the *apportional* type. The *remote* grandparents did not derive much meaning from either source. *Symbolic* grandparents were those who derived little meaning from personal experience and conceived the role in normative terms. The *individualized* grandpar-

Table 6.3.   Age Differences in Styles of Grandparenting[a]

	Under 65 N = 81	Over 65 N = 34
	(percent)	
Formal	31	59
Fun-seeking	37	21
Distant figure	32	21

Source: Adapted from Neugarten and Weinstein, 1964.
[a]These age differences are significant at the .02 level.

Table 6.4. Types of Role Meaning for Grandparents

	Meaning from Personal *Sources*	
	High	*Low*
High	*Apportioned* Grandfathers: 41 Grandmothers: 36	*Symbolic* Grandfathers: 34 Grandmothers: 33
Low	*Individualized* Grandfathers: 22 Grandmothers: 21	*Remote* Grandfathers: 35 Grandmothers: 35

Source: From Jaber F. Gubrium, *Time, Roles and Self in Old Age,* Human Sciences Press, 1976. Used by permission.

ents are those who are high on the personal dimension and low on the social dimension.

Grandparents in the *apportioned* and *individualized* groups, who derived most of the meaning of the relationship with their grandchildren from personal relationships, were significantly older than those who did not get personal satisfactions. They engaged in more activities with their grandchildren, perhaps because fewer were still employed.

Among the younger grandparents who were low on the personal dimension, those classified as *remote* engaged in significantly fewer activities with grandchildren than those classified as *symbolic*—despite the fact that on the average they had more grandchildren. Not surprisingly, there was a significant association between the number of activities with grandchildren and the emphasis on personal significance of grandparenthood. Thus, the higher the number of grandparental activities, the higher the score on the personal dimension. This finding, of course, does not specify which is cause and which is consequence.

Compared to grandparents with lower activity involvement with grandchildren, those with greater interaction had more grandchildren on the average. They had become grandparents at a younger age and were also older at the time of the study.

The most important finding of this research was that the levels of grandparent role activities were not related significantly to life satisfaction, which was tied instead to friendship and organizational activities. Wood and Robertson noted: "This supports Blau's contention (1973) that an older person who has a single good friend is more able to cope with old age than one who has a dozen grandchildren but no peer-group friends" (1976, p. 299).

Although involvement in the grandparent role (as measured by activities with grandchildren) is not significantly related to general life satisfaction, the role is still important to many older people. Grandparents expect their grandchildren to show some measure of interest and concern. Many are content to engage in a variety of activities with grandchildren at least several times a year: visits to the zoo, movies, playing with them, babysitting, giving them gifts, reading to them, and the like.

Data that highlight the problems of generalizing from self-reports come from a direct observational study by Scott (1962). When she got together three generations in an experimental situation where the amounts and kinds of interpersonal interaction were observed (grandmothers, both parents, and a teenage grandchild), the grandmother proved to be singularly unimportant in the interpersonal interactions of the parents and their child. It may be that the grandparent/grandchild interaction is higher with younger grandchildren, as some researchers conclude, or that it is a secondary kind of interaction that takes on vigor only when the intervening generation is passive or not present.

Actually, most researchers have focused upon the grandmother role. We need more attention focused upon grandfathers. Will men who were highly involved in the parental role as fathers, rather than just as providers, be more highly involved in the grandfather and great-grandfather roles? Do grandfathers increase their involvement with grandchildren after they retire? What effect does widowhood have upon involvement in the grandparent role? We still do not know whether the grandparent role becomes more salient with age, or after people become retired or widowed. Robertson (1977) found that grandmothers' role behavior primarily involves babysitting, home recreation, and drop-in visits—mostly initiated by the parent or grandchild. Is this also true for grandfathers?

In summary, the research findings to date suggest that the grandparent role is not a highly significant one for most older people, but that for a few older people it is very meaningful and a great source of personal satisfaction.

Great-Grandparents

About 40 percent of the older people in the United States are great-grandparents. This role, much more clearly than the grandparent one, involves very old people with very young children. This can create problems, because young children, particularly American children, are highly active and may irritate very old people with their impatience.

While there are many four-generation families, little attention has been paid to this phenomenon. We know something about mutual aid patterns in multigenerational families, but we know very little about the psychological and sociological consequences of having a four-generation family, particularly in terms of intergenerational relationships, although Bekker and Taylor (1966) found that young people with living grandparents and great-grandparents tended to be less prejudiced than others against older people.

Great-grandparenthood has been mentioned incidentally, if at all, in most research. For example Boyd (1969b), stated that great-grandparents want and appreciate love and affection. In Wood and Robertson's (1976) working-class sample of 257 grandparents, about 30 percent of the women and 20 percent of the men had great-grandchildren. Yet the focus of the research was upon the meaning and significance of grandparenthood, not great-grandparenthood.

It has been noted that we do not know whether people shift their identity to that of great-grandparents as their grandchildren become parents (Wood and Robertson, 1976). Neither do we know whether people become more involved with their children's grandchildren and less involved with their own grandchildren. How do great-grandparents allocate their time and themselves in their various family roles?

Summary

Most of what we know about grandparents is about grandmothers. They tend now to be middle-aged rather than "old," to be employed and involved in their own lives rather than highly involved with their grandchildren or great-grandchildren. Their relations with their grandchildren are contingent upon their relations with their own children in most cases, and where there is high involvement with children—particularly along the female line—there is also relatively high involvement with grandchildren.

Chapter Seven

Siblings and Other Kin

Siblings

Almost all of the surprisingly sparse literature on sibling relations deals only with childhood. Yet there are many interesting questions relevant to all times of life. For example, how many older Americans have living brothers and sisters? How many live near each other? How frequently do they maintain contact through visits, phone calls, and letter writing? Are adult siblings considered important at holidays and family ritual occasions (weddings, funerals, reunions, and so on)? Do they help each other with financial aid, services, and advice? How do older people feel about their brothers and sisters? Do they maintain previous patterns of allegiance, solidarity, or rivalry, or do their relationships change over the life course? Do they grow closer or farther apart? If so, why? In spite of this list of questions, most writers on the aging family mention siblings just in passing or include them among the category of *other relatives*. Here is another area where we desperately need research.

Prevalence

About 80 percent of older Americans have at least one living sibling. A 1975 study involving a national sample of people over sixty-five indicated that 81 percent had children, 79 percent had siblings, 75 percent had grandchildren, and 4 percent had living parents (Harris and Associates, 1975). Thus, siblings are as available as children, at least in the oldest American cohorts. Similar figures on sibling availability have been found in smaller samples. Shanas et al. (1968) point out that over half of women over sixty-five have a husband alive but six in seven have a sibling alive. Siblings are more available to women than are spouses. In San Francisco, people over sixty-five (Clark and Anderson, 1967) have more sibs than any other relatives alive—38 percent spouses, 61 percent children, and 93 percent sibs. In a Kentucky sample of older people (Youmans, 1963), 80 percent had living children and 82 percent living sibs. Clark and Anderson (1967) found that the most common kinship role among their sample of older people was that of sibling. The number of children per family, however, has been dropping steadily over the past century, so that younger cohorts of adults (ages forty through sixty-five, for example) may not have as many brothers and sisters as the previous generations. And even though people now middle-aged are still likely to have some living siblings, fewer of the cohorts now in their early youth will.

In spite of the presence of siblings, frequent contact with them is less common for older people than with ascendant/descendant (parent/child) relatives. Harris and Associates (1975) found that 44 percent of older people all over the United States had seen a sibling within the last week or two, compared to 81 percent who had seen a child. In general, most data show about twice as much contact with children and parents as with sibs (Shanas, 1973).

As for other kin-keeping data, women are more likely than men to maintain frequent contact with sibs, their own and their in-laws.

Relationships

Shanas et al. (1968) saw siblings as part of the *reservoir* of collateral relatives from which substitutes for more direct kin—that is, those in the ascendant/descendant line—could be drawn. A different point of view was given by Cumming and Henry (1961), unfortunately on the basis of very sparse data. They saw *sibling solidarity* as a special case of generational solidarity, and believed that sibling solidarity takes on new importance in middle age. Cumming and Henry (1961), when they considered the possibility of substitution for lost kin, reported that friends take the place of lost siblings more than of lost children. They concluded that the parent/child bond is dependent in nature, but the sib bond is between equals and thus more like friendship. If for no other reason, sibs' availability could make them an important source of family interaction in later life. Parron (1978) found that her small sample of golden wedding couples seemed to have almost as much contact with siblings as with children, some of the women "being on the phone" with them almost every day.

With the advent of old age, many older people may seek to pick up old family loyalties and renew old relationships. More effort may be made to visit siblings, even at great distances, after retirement and corresponding disengagement from other social roles, than in middle age. The narrower the older person's social world, the more likely she or he is spontaneously to mention a sibling as a source of aid in time of trouble or need. Next to adult children, siblings are the best prospects for providing older people with a permanent home. Except in those cases which involve long-term family feuds, siblings offer a logical source of primary relationships, particularly for older people whose primary bonds have been reduced by death of a spouse or distancing of children. Shanas et al. (1968) report that siblings are particularly important in the lives of never-married older persons. The death of a sibling, particularly when the relationship was a close one, may shock a person more than the death of any other kin. Since they are of the same family *and* generation, their death apparently brings home one's own mortality with great immediacy.

Although some writers (Shanas et al., 1968; Cumming and Schneider, 1961) believe there is a positive relationship between age and sibling solidarity, others have found lowered rates of sibling interaction following the death of parents—particularly mothers (Young and Willmott, 1957; Adams, 1968a), and particularly among *older* urban working-class people (Rosenberg and Anspach, 1973). Thus, working-class people in Philadelphia aged sixty-five and over were less likely to interact with available siblings than those aged forty-five to sixty-four. This negative relation between age and interaction was even stronger for own siblings than for spouse's siblings (sisters-in-law and brothers-in-law). Beyond this age relation, Rosenberg and Anspach (1973) found comparatively low sibling interaction among working-class people of all ages, except for those whose marriages had been disrupted.

"Old people who have never married tend to maintain much closer relationships with their brothers and sisters than those who marry and have children. Persons without children tend to resume closer associations with siblings upon the death of a spouse, but interestingly, not as close as single persons" (Shanas et al., 1968). Following the principle of female linkage observed in other kinship attachments, sister/sister ties have been observed to be stronger than sister/brother ties with brother/brother ties generally the weakest (Cumming and Schneider, 1961; Irish, 1964; Adams, 1968a; Reiss, 1962).

Cross-sectional data (alluded to several times in this book) from four stages in the life span (Lowenthal et al., 1975) indicated fewer *stage* differences in perceptions of siblings than in perceptions of parents or children. There was also little sex difference in perceptions of siblings. Unlike the findings of several other studies, these San Franciscans were more positive in their evaluations of cross-sex siblings than of same-sex siblings (at all the life stages). As noted in earlier chapters, strong bonds can be expressed as hate as well as love; this hypothesis, however, has not yet been tested, particularly for siblings. Again, San Franciscans may have different family relationships from samples in other parts of the country.

Discussions of sibling relations in later life will remain speculative until more data are available. It seems likely that continuity in sibling relations is more common than not. In cases where a relationship has been competitive in childhood, sibs are probably used as standards for comparison throughout the life course (Adams, 1968a). One's progress or success or that of one's children can be compared to that of siblings or their children.

Other Kin

The same principles that are said to operate with respect to siblings apply to other *collateral kin* such as cousins, aunts, uncles, nieces, and nephews. First, they serve as a reservoir of kin from which replacement and substitutions for missing or lost relatives can be obtained. From among this pool of more distant relatives, ties would be based upon individual characteristics more than on closeness of kinship. The scattered bits of research about such kin are seldom based upon "favorite cousin" or "favorite uncle or niece," but rather upon "best-known cousin" (Adams, 1968a); or a male cousin, mother's oldest brother, father's oldest brother (Klatsky, 1972); or "extended family" (Brown, 1974), to cite a few examples.

For most people, *extended kin* become temporarily important at family ritual occasions such as weddings, funerals, reunions, and some holidays. These symbolic significances can override interpersonal feelings, which probably depend upon personal characteristics and history. Positional symbolic representation can be in terms of a particular family line or even of a generation. Thus, a relative will be invited to a wedding to represent the bridegroom's paternal family or to represent the oldest living generation. When grandparents die, great-aunts or great-uncles are invited to give the family a more rounded presence.

Lineal kin (parents and children) maintain contact in spite of distance, but more distant relatives are probably estranged more easily by geographic distance. Cousins, however, may see each other frequently when they visit their own parents who are siblings living in the same community, and other distant kin can become close if they move nearby.

There are several data sources on extended family from the perspective of young adult populations, but few from that of older people. Thus, Robins and Tomanec (1962) found that young adults (both males and females) were closer to their maternal than to paternal relatives, and closer to female than to male relatives. After parents and siblings, they were closest to (1) grandparents, (2) aunts and uncles, and then (3) cousins. Adams's (1968a) sample from Greensboro, whose median age was about thirty-three, showed a similar order of importance. We can conclude from this and other research that interaction with secondary kin depends upon geographic proximity *and* preference. Thus, geographic distance does not necessarily lead to kin isolation.

Nearly 70 percent of the people over fifty-five in Brown's (1974) sample said they had experienced no change in contact with extended family members during the previous decade. Brown found that although older people do not disengage from children when relationships are not satisfactory, they do disengage from extended family interactions when satisfaction is low. (However, only 13 percent said that their extended kin relationships were less than ideal.) Those people who had low extended family contacts made them up by other social contacts.

In another study with a sample of inner-city elderly, 15 percent reported that relatives were an income source (Walters and Mitchell, 1974, 38). Most people believe that their relatives (as compared with neighbors or friends) would help in *emergency* situations lasting one day, two weeks, and three months (Litwak and Szelenyi, 1969). Unfortunately, this generic term *relatives,* used in much of gerontological research, does not distinguish among children, siblings, and other kin.

Middle-class people visit their relatives more than working-class people do, if geographic distance is controlled. Middle-class kin also tend to be more dispersed geographically than working-class kin. Thus, it is in spite of greater distances that middle-class families maintain contact. Among working-class older people, the rate of interaction with both genealogically close and distant kin is largely a function of geographic proximity (Rosenberg, 1970). Restricted contact with kin in later life is also partially related to a history of income deprivation and consequent restricted mobility.

Gibson (1972), surveying a sample of *disabled* middle-aged and older people—those who had applied for OASDI (Old Age and Survivors Disability Insurance)—used a somewhat different form of reporting frequency. Of 5.7 nonhousehold relatives available (not living with respondent), 0.5 were seen daily, 1.2 weekly, 1.1 monthly, and 2.9 less than monthly. Thus, half were seen monthly, a somewhat larger proportion than found by Reiss (1962) for middle-class Bostonians.

Gibson also found that the proportion of available kin seen at least monthly does not vary with age, and is higher for unmarried than for married people. Thirty-eight percent of these available or existing kin lived in the same community, 51 percent were seen at least monthly, but only 17 percent provided *significant* help. Thus, among these very needy people aged sixty to seventy, 58 percent received no services from their kin. It is noteworthy that the proportion of helpful relatives did not decline with age but, like interaction frequency, was much lower for those still married.

Though rural samples report fewer relatives nearby than urban samples do because of rural to urban population shifts, their visiting patterns with those who are available do not differ significantly from those of urban residents. There is, of course, less frequent *absolute* kin interaction where availability is lower (Britton and Britton, 1967; Bultena, 1969a; and Hawkinson, 1965), but about the same *proportionate* frequency, much of it by telephone (Powers et al., 1975).

Some writers (Cumming and Schneider, 1961; Clark and Anderson, 1967; Gibson, 1972; Arling, 1976; Petrowsky, 1976) include friends as possible substitutes for kin. This may be more relevant in old age, when more kin are lost, than at younger ages. Shanas et al. (1968) found nearly 20 percent of people over sixty-five virtually kinless. Gibson, Arling, and Petrowsky have all noted that friends and neighbors may be more important in aid networks than some existing kin.

In-Laws

Limited attention has been devoted to the *in-law* relationship in the latter part of the family life cycle. Most writers refer only to the in-law adjustment problems of young married couples; few note the adjustment problems of middle-aged parents and even older grandparents to the new families introduced into kin networks upon each new marriage in the family (Troll, 1971a).

Adams (1968a) found that middle-class wives write to both sets of parents, while working-class wives concentrate upon their own kin. Turner (Troll and Turner, 1976) found that her women college students were writing to their lovers' parents and had taken over the female kin-keeping functions way in advance of marriage, even in the presence of doubtful prospects of eventual marriage. Urban working-class people in the last half of the life cycle tend to reduce or lose contacts with brothers- and sisters-in-law when their marriages are disrupted (Lopata, 1973; Rosenberg and Anspach, 1973) either by widowhood or divorce.

At this end of the family life cycle, the relations between a middle-aged woman vis-à-vis her mother and mother-in-law, who both may require help and attention, has been even more ignored than the problems with the new in-laws. How would a lifelong habit of mother-in-law avoidance affect the need to assist in old age? Shanas et al. (1968) report that daughters-in-law do often take over the responsibilities of care for needy older people when no daughters are available. How would this affect the quality of attentions or the feelings of the people involved? Troll and Turner (1976) point to the Cassandra syndrome of the middle-aged woman who is beset with worries about her relatives of all ages, including her in-laws (see discussion in Chapter 3).

Summary

While most older Americans have more living siblings than any other close relative with the possible exception of children, we know remarkably little about sibling relationships in later life. What evidence we do have is contradictory; some studies suggest that siblings grow closer as time goes by, others that they become more distant, particularly after their mother has died. The sex linkage seems to hold true for sibling as well as parent/child relationships, with sister/sister closest, sister/brother next, and brother/brother least. More distant kin—cousins, in-laws, aunts, nephews, and so on—may serve as a reservoir for substitutions for lost closer kin. They may also serve ritual purposes to "round out the family," and, finally, may be regarded for their own personal or historical connections rather than for closeness of kinship.

Chapter Eight

Implications

For People in General

Because most readers are themselves involved in multigeneration families in one way or another, this book can help by identifying common patterns. What has been presented here can be compressed into relatively general statements that can serve as points of departure for *careful observation* of specific situations.

In relating to older family members, remember that aging does not dissolve a person's attitudes and preferences. Particularly in *assisting* older people, remember that they want to preserve every ounce of autonomy, independence, and self-respect possible. Most older people do not want to depend on their children more than they must, and they especially do not want to live in three-generation households. Fortunately, most get what they want.

As long as older people are part of a marital couple, they usually take care of one another's needs for assistance. But unmarried older people are more likely to look to their children, or to other relatives if they are childless. Providing assistance to older family members who value independence can be tricky; the assister must inject himself or herself into the decision making as little as possible. Older people often feel guilty about having to ask for assistance.

On the other hand, probably the hardest thing to do is to relate to older family members *as they are now* rather than as they were in the past. It can be very hard to change patterns of interaction and perception, although in the long run it can prevent many unrealistic decisions. It is important, therefore, to pay close attention to what older people see as their needs for assistance—exactly what problem they think needs solving and how they want to solve it. It's easier to negotiate differences beforehand than to try to backtrack later.

It is also important not to try to take over problems and problem solving. Well-meaning people constantly tell older people by their actions—taking over—that they consider the older person incapable of dealing with his or her own decisions. Such behavior can become a self-fulfilling prophecy. If older people are reduced to helplessness by the intrusion of others, however well meaning, they can become truly unable to care for themselves. By the same token, encouraging apparently helpless older persons to make many of their own decisions can help them become more competent and independent.

If older family members are respected and treated as fully competent adults, all members of the family profit. The more we value older family members, the more we can value ourselves. If older family members want to behave badly or irresponsibly—though few of them do—then that is *their* choice to make. Another good rule to follow: If you are going to give advice, you must be prepared for others not to take it.

These general orientations, plus the general summaries given throughout the book, should serve as a solid starting point in observing your relationships with older members of your own family.

For Counseling or Psychotherapy

The focus of most practitioners in the helping professions is on individuals who can be treated in *direct,* one-way interactions: from helping persons to helped persons. This is true of children, adults, or older people. Whether the treatment is primarily *indirect* intervention—as tends more to be the case for older people—or some kind of "therapy," it seldom takes into consideration all the concurrent interactions between the clients and their relatives. The purpose of this present section is to point out some implications for treating such inter-relationships.

For Treating Children

At the present time, as the data presented earlier in this book attest, most children are raised in families with fewer siblings and more grandparents and great-grandparents than were their parents or grandparents in their own childhood. Although these grandparents today are not likely to be living in the same household, they *are* likely to be close by. Furthermore, many children are not only involved with grandparents but also with other relatives such as aunts and uncles and cousins. If the present trend toward more people's living to old age should continue, there could be even more three- or four-generation families in the future than there are now. Family relationships could thus become even more complex. In addition, the increasing rates of divorce and remarriage can multiply the number of parents and of half-siblings, and also—and this has less often been mentioned— grandparents and uncles and aunts and cousins. Should the present high frequency of teenage parenting continue to rise, furthermore, the time span between family generations could get shorter than the current twenty years, and families of five or six generations could become the rule instead of three or four—that is, if the other current trend to continue to postpone childrearing does not lead instead to fewer generations. Based on the discussion in Chapter 5, we would also expect that the increasing proportion of unmarried parents would be associated with closer ties between them and their own parents, thus bringing extended kin more into the childrearing picture than they would be in intact families. We know so little about kinship relations among reconstituted families that we cannot even speculate about them. Finally, we must consider not only these trends but also the fact that, in the American population as a whole, not only has the number of children per couple decreased, but there are proportionately fewer people between twenty and thirty-five and more older people (Hauser, 1976).

The presence of multiple generations in the world of the growing child may not provide more caretaking, since grandparents as well as parents could be busy "doing their own thing." It is likely, however, to provide an array of interested people with complex interrelationships who would serve as models of diversity in lifestyle and of diversity in interrelationships. Many of these adults would definitely care about whether the children are doing the "right" things. What that will mean for the children in terms of their needing more professional help is hard to say. But we could be fairly confident in predicting that any practitioners who deal with children as if they are isolated from all relatives but their mothers are likely to be losing fertile sources of aid as well as misperceiving the children's background situation and thus misdiagnosing and treating incorrectly. On the other side of the coin, those children who turn out to be indeed isolated from extended kin should probably be evaluated as more unusual than they might be according to the norms of the isolated nuclear family. Parents who are separated not only from each other but from their own parents or siblings represent such a small proportion of the population that practitioners who treat children from such isolated surroundings should be alerted to possible deeper and longer-lasting problems over several generations. Thus, counselors or therapists need to avoid two opposite types of error: (1) assuming that their child clients have no kin (other than perhaps mothers) or (2) assuming that their child clients who have no kin are from "normal" family patterns.

Marital Counseling

Husbands and wives who have no children—or only one or two—are freer to pursue activities other than childrearing, including their own relationship. This could lead alternatively to greater demands for pleasure and satisfaction from marriage, to quicker consideration of divorce when pleasure and satisfaction do not meet expectations, or to lessened attention to spouse when other activities are salient. These patterns contrast with those of parents who are busy with many young children and who must work together as partners for the sake of their commitment to bringing up "good" children. The latter kinds of marriage partners are not as likely to continue to emphasize the intense one-to-one relationship of their honeymoon or pre-children period—though some may revert to it once their children are grown.

Couples seeking counseling in later life could therefore be of two types: those who have developed along different paths over the years or those whose previous partnership interactions have proved no longer appropriate. Couples could differ in another parameter as well: those who value self-actualization over familism and those who value familism more. In Chapter 3, we suggested that the quality of marital interaction could change over the years from intense *attraction*-oriented feelings in the beginning of marriage to less intense *attachment*-oriented feelings later. Evidence that some couples who have been married many years find loyalty and emotional security rewarding, as well as other evidence that suggests that some couples experience increased enjoyment of sex and intimacy when their children leave, should all be considered in discussing options and prospects. Those couples that foresee the benefits of loyalty and emotional security may decide their marriage is worth keeping even if the early excitement has disappeared. Those that do not, however, may seek new partners or new activities, although they must keep in mind that men may find it easier to get new partners and women new activities. It is possible that *open marriage* is better suited to couples married twenty years or more than to newlyweds, particularly where self-actualization is valued.

Helping older couples become aware of their implicit values and the options these entail is only part of the implications of this book. Appropriate treatment or intervention could lead to renewed vigor of old relationships. Awareness of the possibility of continued sexuality into late life and an equal awareness of prevailing myths of sexuality ending with the climacteric are necessary. Even though divorce may now have reached the status of a new norm in some circles, it need not be the only option for unhappy older couples.

Marital counselors often focus on the relationship of the husband and wife alone. The thrust of this book should alert them also to consider children and parents—even if the children are grown. It is clear that a commitment to self-actualization or self-fulfillment can run counter to commitments to kin which, since they are long-standing and powerful, may produce emotional havoc.

Sex differences enter the picture at all points, from income consequences, health and length of life differentials, social role expectations, household division of labor, and remarriage possibilities. Any counselor who ignores them—or ethnic or social class differences as well—is in danger of making incorrect assumptions about the condition of couples he or she is helping. The apparent concomitants of successful remarriages and also the possibilities for life satisfaction as unmarried people in old age are other important kinds of information counselors need.

Adult Child/Older Parent Treatment

In the normal course of events, parenting continues to be an important preoccupation of older people even when their children are grown; and in the normal course of events, children continue to interact with and exchange services with their parents after they are themselves adults. Events are not always "normal," however, and previous chapters do show that where older parents—or for that matter their children—are in trouble, they look to and receive most of their help from each other.

People in the helping professions tend to have certain biases which may interfere with or ignore such commonly held tendencies. They may make plans for older people which ignore the fact that most have children who care what happens to them. They may believe that children do not—or should not—care for their older parents. In Chapter 5 we discussed some of the qualitative aspects of parent/child relationships in later life. Some parents and their children may have been estranged for many years. Others may have very strong feelings of either love or hate or both, as well as strong familial values which include feelings of shame or guilt or obligations that need to be considered. The fact that no more than 5 percent of all older people in the United States reside in any kind of institutional setting—nursing homes, long-term care facilities, "senior" residences—speaks for itself. Counselors need to explore the nature of individual relationships involved and possibilities for a variety of care options. Since many older parents value independence and autonomy, and get more satisfaction from the success of their children than their care or availability, they may be afraid of being a burden upon their children or of causing the relationship with them to deteriorate. Thus, they might make decisions based upon such fears which are harder for their children to take than their need for help.

For the Academic Community

Students and *teachers* will notice many areas of this book where the references indicate that enough research has been done to allow in-depth student papers. Because our summaries are necessarily selective, it is advisable to go to the primary sources for a more in-depth look at the various topics. In researching papers, students would be well advised to keep in mind the issues, perspectives, and problems raised in Chapter 2. This chapter, combined with the material on each of the substantive topics, provides a good vantage point for beginning a term paper. Of course, by the time this book is published, numerous new studies will have appeared that should be incorporated.

Researchers should find this book a help in identifying and clarifying many theoretical, conceptual, and methodological issues in studying families in later life. In addition, the text points out numerous areas where more research is needed. In particular, more research is needed that uses the older couple—both members—as the unit to be studied. Chapter 3 catalogs numerous issues such as changes in the quality of relationship, values, division of labor, and decisions about organizing time and space that have received scant attention in research on older couples. More research is needed that studies several members of the *extended family networks* of older people, particularly those who are unmarried. In general, there has been too little emphasis on the dynamics—the ebb and flow—of family relationships. These are just a few of dozens of topics that need more research. This is indeed a promising area for researchers looking for new avenues to explore.

For Public Policy

Much of this book has implications mainly for individual family members and those who work with them. There are some implications for public policy, however, that seem worth considering.

Public policy should not attempt to force older people to be dependent on their adult children. Laws that require children to be financially responsible for parents have never worked well and have generally been abandoned.

Public policy should recognize, however, that society benefits from financial contributions adult children make to their older parents. For example, in 1978 let us suppose that a son contributes $3000 in cash toward the support of his widowed mother, who lives in her own apartment. She also receives $240 per month social security, a total of $2880 for the year. Medicare, Part A, paid for a period of hospitalization to the tune of $435. Internal Revenue counts Medicare as "support" to the mother; and her total "support" for the year is $6315. Because he did not contribute more than half of his mother's "support," the son cannot claim her as a dependent on his taxes. It would be more fair if the son could simply pay the $3000 to his mother, have *her* count it as taxable income for the year, and let him deduct the $3000 from his gross income. But Internal Revenue does not allow that. Thus, not only must the son pay the $3000 directly for his mother, he also must pay $1000 in taxes as part of the "support" he gave his mother. The end result is that the son is out $1000 in taxes on income he never saw; he gets no income tax relief for assisting his mother. But if he had paid an older woman he had never seen before $3000 to watch cars go by and she had no other taxable income, she would not have to pay any taxes on the income, and he would be able to deduct the entire $3000 from his gross taxable income. This is a fine example of the maxim, "No good deed ever goes unpunished."

Public policy should take family patterns of interaction into account. For example, current housing policies emphasize construction of new multiple-unit dwellings for older people. This policy completely ignores the fact that both older parents and their adult children would prefer retaining the family home. Rehabilitation, repair, and services for detached homes is not a part of our strategy for housing older Americans, despite an overwhelming preference, and usually a lower price tag, for this type of approach. Because direct federal dollars and federally insured mortgage dollars are not currently going into renovation or repair of existing homes, a well-organized industry to implement this more conservation-minded housing strategy does not exist. This is an example of multiple federal policies that put pressure on older people to leave their homes, sometimes disrupting longstanding patterns of kinship (and neighborhood) interaction. Thanksgiving dinner at the housing project is just not the same as Thanksgiving "at home."

Public income policy should recognize that although most retired couples live together in a single household, this is not always the case. For example, Jay and Em were both seventy-three and had a retirement income of about $650 per month, which supported them quite well. However, Em had a stroke and that left her completely dependent—far beyond Jay's capacity to care for her. Jay had Em entered into the least expensive skilled nursing home in the area, where the cost of care was $675 per month. Obviously, Jay is not going to be able to afford this when Em's days of coverage under Medicare run out. What does he do, besides worry? This is an important policy issue. Retirement incomes that support couples quite nicely are often inadequate if the income must be divided to support two levels of care.

The foregoing examples do not exhaust the list of public policy implications of this book, and the reader is invited to think of others. They do illustrate what can happen when current public policies are examined in relation to what real life is like.

Epilogue

The use of families as resources to fill the financial, physical, mental, and emotional needs of older members is viewed from two opposing perspectives. One perspective suggests that services and care should be provided by the state or by other organizations that use trained personnel and so are likely to be more skilled than unskilled family members. This may be particularly true for medical care. This perspective suggests that we may be expecting too much from the family. Not all family members have a high level of affection and concern for the welfare of other members. In some families, particularly those in which resources are limited and needs great, attention may focus on younger rather than older members. The strain of trying to meet everybody's needs may be too great for such families to handle. According to this perspective, then, we should not view the family as a "dumping ground" for older people, particularly since some older people are without kin.

The opposing perspective suggests that the services and care provided by relatives for older people are more personal and thus of higher quality than organizational services and care. This viewpoint holds that we now expect too little from the family and that many needs could be satisfied by kin if society would provide additional support. This perspective would support subsidies to family members who provide services or care to kin and would encourage the integration of families into nursing home activities and services.

At the societal level these perspectives involve the social, political, and economic questions of who should be responsible for older people who have unmet needs—the state or the family—and where governmental resources should be allocated. At the individual level the question of personal costs and benefits to the older people and each of their relatives becomes important.

When an older family member who needs care and services resides in a household rather than in an institution, the financial cost of that care is usually borne by the family. Attempts are being made to calculate and compare the cost effectiveness of at-home care and institutional care. We may then see some changes in policy to provide financial help for families that do care for aged members at home. But before the pendulum swings all the way, we urge that the emotional and psychic costs and benefits be considered as well as the financial costs and benefits.

We believe that public policies which maximize alternative options are the most desirable. Given the great diversity of lifestyles and preferences in society today, no single-faceted program can serve the needs of everyone.

References

Adams, Bert N.
1964   "Structural factors affecting parental aid to kin." Journal of Mar-
            riage and the Family 26:327–31.
1967a   "Interaction theory and the social network." Sociometry 30:64–
            78.
1967b   "Occupational position, mobility, and the kin of orientation."
            American Sociological Review 32:364–77.
1968a   Kinship in an Urban Setting. Chicago: Markham.
1968b   "The middle-class adult and his widowed or still-married mother."
            Social Problems 16:51–59.
1971   "Isolation, function, and beyond: American kinship in the
            1960's." In Carlfred Broderick (ed.), A Decade of Family Re-
            search and Action. Minneapolis: Council on Family Relations.
1975   "Aging and the family in the United States." In Bert N. Adams
            (ed.), The Family: A Sociological Interpretation. 2nd ed. Chicago:
            Rand McNally.
Ahammer, I. M. and P. B. Baltes
1972   "Objective versus perceived age differences in personality; how
            do adolescents, adults, and older people view themselves and each
            other?" Journal of Gerontology 27:46–51.
Albrecht, Ruth
1962   "The role of older people in family rituals." In Clark Tibbetts and
            Wilma Donahue (eds.), Social and Psychological Aspects of Ag-
            ing. Aging Around the World. New York: Columbia University
            Press.
1969   "The family and aging seen cross-culturally." In Rosamonde R.
            Boyd and Charles G. Oakes (eds.), Foundations of Practical
            Gerontology. Columbia, S.C.: University of South Carolina
            Press.
Aldous, Joan
1965   "The consequences of inter-generational continuity." Journal of
            Marriage and the Family 27:462–68.

1967   "Intergenerational visiting patterns: Variation in boundary maintenance as an explanation." Family Process 6(2):235–51.

Aldous, Joan and Reuben Hill
1965   "Social cohesion, lineage type, and intergenerational transmission." Social Forces 43:471–82.
1967   International Bibliography of Research in Marriage and the Family 1900–1964. Distributed by the University of Minnesota Press for the Minnesota Family Study Center and the Institute of Life Insurance.

Aller, Florence A.
1962   "Role of the self-concept in student marital adjustment." Family Life Coordinator (11):43–45.

Angres, Salma
1975   "Intergenerational relations and value congruence between young adults and their mothers." Unpublished doctoral dissertation, University of Chicago.

Apple, Dorrian
1956   "The social structure of grandparenthood." American Anthropologist 58:656–63.

Arling, Greg
1976   "The elderly widow and her family, neighbors, and friends." Journal of Marriage and the Family 38(3):757–68.

Atchley, Robert C.
1971   "Disengagement among professors." Journal of Gerontology 26:476–80.
1975a   "Sex differences among middle-class retired people." In Robert C. Atchley, Research Studies in Social Gerontology. Oxford, Ohio: Scripps Foundation.
1975b   "Dimensions of widowhood in later life." The Gerontologist 15(2):176–78.
1975c   "Adjustment to loss of job at retirement." International Journal of Aging and Human Development 6:17–27.
1976   The Sociology of Retirement. New York: John Wiley & Sons.
1977   Social Forces in Later Life. 2nd ed. Belmont, Ca.: Wadsworth.

Atchley, Robert C. and Sherry Corbett
1977   "Older women and jobs." In Lillian Troll, Joan Israel, and Kenneth Israel (eds.), Looking Ahead: A Woman's Guide to the Problems and Joys of Growing Older. Englewood Cliffs, N.J.: Prentice-Hall.

Atchley, Robert C. and Sheila J. Miller
1975   "Housing and the rural aged." In Robert C. Atchley (ed.), Environments and the Rural Aged. Washington D.C.: Gerontological Society.

Atchley, Robert C., Linda Pignatiello, and Ellen Shaw
1975   "The effect of marital status on social interaction patterns of older women." Oxford, Ohio: Scripps Foundation.

Axelson, Leland L.
1960   "Personal adjustments in the postparental period." Marriage and Family Living 22:66–70.

Ayoub, Millicent R.
1966   "The family reunion." Ethnology 5(4):415–33.
Back, Kurt W.
1965   "A social psychologist looks at kinship structure." In Ethel
            Shanas and Gordon Streib (eds.), Social Structure and the Family:
            Generational Relations. Englewood Cliffs, N.J.: Prentice-Hall.
Bahr, S. J.
1973   "Effects of power and division of labor on the family." In Lois W.
            Hoffman and Gerald I. Nye (eds.), Working Mothers. San Fran-
            cisco: Jossey-Bass.
Ballweg, John A.
1967   "Resolution of conjugal role adjustment after retirement." Journal
            of Marriage and the Family 29:277–81.
Bart, Pauline B.
1971   "Depression in middle-aged women." In V. Gornick and B. K.
            Moran (eds.), Women in Sexist Society. New York: Basic Books.
Bekker, L. de Moyne and Charles Taylor
1966   "Attitudes toward aging in a multigenerational sample." Journal of
            Gerontology 21:115–18.
Belcher, John C.
1967   "A consequence of the isolated nuclear family." Journal of Mar-
            riage and the Family 29:534–40.
Bell, Bill D.
1973   "The family life cycle, primary relationships, and social participa-
            tion patterns." The Gerontologist 13:78–81.
Bell, Robert
1965   "The lower class Negro mother's aspirations for her children."
            Social Forces 43(4):493–500.
Bell, Robert R.
1971   Marriage and Family Interaction. 3rd ed. Homewood, Ill.: Dorsey
            Press.
1975   Marriage and Family Interaction. 4th ed. Homewood, Ill.: Dorsey
            Press.
Bellin, Seymour S. and Robert H. Hardt
1958   "Marital status and mental disorders of the aged." American
            Sociological Review 23:155–62.
Bengtson, Vern L.
1970   "The generation gap: A review and typology of social-
            psychological perspectives." Youth and Society 2(1):7–32.
1971   "Inter-age perceptions and the generation gap." The Geron-
            tologist 11(4, part 2):85–89.
Bengtson, Vern L. and K. D. Black
1973   "Intergenerational relations and continuities in socialization." In
            P. B. Baltes and K. W. Schaie (eds.), Life-Span Developmental
            Psychology. Personality and Socialization. New York: Academic
            Press.
Bengtson, Vern L. and Joseph A. Kuypers
1971   "Generational difference and the developmental stake." Aging
            and Human Development 2:249–60.

Bengtson, Vern L., E. Olander, and A. Haddad
1976   "The 'generation gap' and aging family members: Toward a conceptual model." In J. F. Gubrium (ed.), Time, Roles, and Self in Old Age. New York: Human Sciences Press.
Berardo, Felix M.
1966   "Kinship interaction and migrant adaptation in an aerospace related community." Journal of Marriage and the Family 28:296–304.
1967a   "Internal migrants and extended family relations: A study of newcomer adaptation in the Cape Kennedy region." Research Reports in Social Science 10(2):23–50.
1967b   "Kinship interaction and communications among space-age migrants." Journal of Marriage and the Family 29:541–54.
1968   "Widowhood status in the U.S.: Perspectives on a neglected aspect of the family life cycle." The Family Coordinator 17:191–203.
1970   "Survivorship and social isolation: The case of the aged widower." The Family Coordinator 19(1):11–25.
Berardo, Felix M. (ed.)
1972   "Aging and the family." Special issue, The Family Coordinator 21(1).
Bernard, Jessie
1973   The Future of Marriage. New York: Bantam Books.
Bettelheim, Bruno
1962   "The problem of generations." Daedalus 91(1):68–96.
Binstock, Robert and Ethel Shanas (eds.)
1976   Handbook of Aging and the Social Sciences. New York: Van Nostrand Reinhold.
Blau, Zena S.
1961   "Structural constraints on friendship in old age." American Sociological Review 26:429–39.
1973   Old Age in a Changing Society. New York: Franklin Watts.
Blenkner, Margaret
1965   "Social work and family relationships in later life with some thoughts on filial maturity." In Ethel Shanas and Gordon F. Streib (eds.), Social Structure and the Family. Englewood Cliffs, N.J.: Prentice-Hall.
1969   "The normal dependencies of aging." In Richard Kalish (ed.), The Dependencies of Old People. Ann Arbor, Mich.: University of Michigan Institute of Gerontology.
Blood, Robert O. and Donald M. Wolfe
1960   Husbands and Wives. New York: The Free Press.
Bloom, Martin and Alexander Monro
1972   "Social work and the aging family." The Family Coordinator 21(1):71–80.
Bohannon, P.
1971   "Dyad dominance and household maintenance." In F. L. K. Hau (ed.), Kinship and Culture. Chicago: Aldine.
Booth, A. and H. Camp
1974   "Housing relocation and family social integration patterns." American Institute of Planners Journal 40:124–28.

Borke, Helen
1963   "Continuity and change in the transmission of adaptive patterns
            over two generations." Marriage and Family Living 25(3):294–99.
1967   "A family over three generations: The transmission of interacting
            and relating patterns." Journal of Marriage and the Family
            29(4):639–55.
Bornstein, P. E. et al.
1973   "The depression of widowhood after thirteen months." British
            Journal of Psychiatry 122:561–66.
Boyd, Rosamonde R.
1969a   "Emerging roles of the four-generation family." In Rosamonde R.
            Boyd and Charles G. Oakes (eds.), Foundations of Practical
            Gerontology. Columbia, S.C.: University of South Carolina
            Press.
1969b   "The valued grandparent: A changing social role." In Wilma
            Donahue (ed.), Living in the Multigenerational Family. Ann Ar-
            bor, Mich.: University of Michigan, Wayne State University Insti-
            tute of Gerontology.
Bracey, H. E.
1966   In Retirement: Pensioners in Great Britain and the United States.
            Baton Rouge: Louisiana State University Press.
Brayshaw, A. Joseph
1962   "Middle-aged marriage: Idealism, realism and a search for mean-
            ing." Marriage and Family Living 24(4):358–64.
Brim, Orville and Stanton Wheeler
1966   Socialization after Childhood. New York: John Wiley & Sons.
Britton, Joseph H. and Jean O. Britton
1967   "The middle-aged and older rural person and his family." In E.
            Grant Youmans (ed.), Older Rural Americans, Lexington, Ky.:
            University of Kentucky.
Britton, Joseph H., William G. Mather, and Alice K. Lansing
1961   "Expectations for older persons in a rural community: Living ar-
            rangements and family relationships." Journal of Gerontology
            16(2):156–62.
Broderick, Carlfred
1971   "Beyond the five conceptual frameworks: A decade of develop-
            ment in family theory." In Carlfred Broderick (ed.), A Decade of
            Family Research and Action. Minneapolis: National Council on
            Family Relations.
Brody, Elaine M.
1963   "The transition from extended families to nuclear families." In
            Richard H. Williams, Clark Tibbitts, and Wilma Donahue (eds.),
            Processes of Aging. Vol. 2. New York: Atherton Press.
1966   "Aging as a family crisis: Implications for research and planning."
            In Proceedings of the Seventh International Congress of Geron-
            tology. Vol. 7. Vienna: Wiener Medizinischen Akadamie.
Brown, Arnold S.
1974   "Satisfying relationships for the elderly and their patterns of dis-
            engagement." The Gerontologist 14:258–62.

Brubaker, Timothy H.
1975   "Marital satisfaction and the retirement stage: A review and theoretical formulation." Paper presented at 1975 National Council on Family Relations Meeting, Salt Lake City, Utah, August 20–23.
Bultena, Gordon L.
1969a   "Rural-urban differences in the familial interaction of the aged." Rural Sociology 34(1):5–15.
1969b   "The relationship of occupational status to friendship ties in three planned retirement communities." Journal of Gerontology 24:461–64.
Bultena, Gordon L. and D. C. Marshall
1970   "Family patterns of migrant and non-migrant retirees." Journal of Marriage and the Family 32:89–93.
Bultena, Gordon L. and Vivian Wood
1969   "The American retirement community: Bane or blessing?" Journal of Gerontology 24:209–17.
Burgess, Ernest W.
1960   "Family structure and relationships." In Ernest W. Burgess (ed.), Aging in Western Societies. Chicago: University of Chicago Press.
Burr, Wesley
1970   "Satisfaction with various aspects of marriage over the life cycle: A random middle-class sample." Journal of Marriage and the Family 32:29–37.
Cameron, P.
1972   "The generation gap; time orientation." The Gerontologist 12:117–19.
Cantor, Marjorie H.
1975   "Life space and the social support system of the inner city elderly of New York." The Gerontologist 15:23–27.
Carp, Frances M. (ed.)
1971   Retirement. New York: Behavioral Publications.
Cash, S. H.
1972   "The geriatric patient and his family. The institutionalization of a parent—a nadir of life." Journal of Geriatric Psychiatry 5:25–46.
Cavan, Ruth S.
1956   "Family tensions between the old and the middle-aged." Marriage and Family Living 18:323–27.
1962   "Self and role in adjustment during old age." In A. M. Rose (ed.), Human Behavior and Social Process, An Interactionist Approach. Boston: Houghton Mifflin.
1963   The American Family. 3rd ed. New York: Thomas Y. Crowell.
Chevan, Albert and J. Henry Korson
1972   "The widowed who live alone: An examination of social and demographic factors. Social Forces 51(1):45–53.
1975   "Living arrangements of widows in the United States and Israel, 1960 and 1961." Demography 12(3):505–18.

Christensen, Harold (ed.)
1964   Handbook of Marriage and the Family. Chicago: Rand McNally.
Christenson, Cornelia V. and John H. Gagnon
1965   "Sexual behavior in a group of older women." Journal of Geron-
            tology 20:351–56.
Christenson, Cornelia V. and A. B. Johnson
1973   "Sexual patterns in a group of older never-married women." Jour-
            nal of Geriatric Psychiatry 6:80–98.
Clark, Margaret
1969   "Cultural values and dependency in later life." In Richard Kalish
            (ed.), The Dependencies of Old People. Ann Arbor, Mich.: Uni-
            versity of Michigan Institute of Gerontology.
Clark, Margaret and Barbara G. Anderson
1967   Culture and Aging. Springfield, Ill.: Charles C. Thomas.
Clavan, S. and E. Vatter
1972   "The affiliated family; a device for integrating old and young."
            The Gerontologist 12:407–12.
Cleveland, William P. and Daniel T. Gianturco
1976   "Remarriage probability after widowhood: A retrospective
            method." Journal of Gerontology 31(1):99–103.
Cottrell, W. Fred and Robert C. Atchley
1969   Women in Retirement: A Preliminary Report. Oxford, Ohio:
            Scripps Foundation.
Cuber, John F. and Peggy Harroff
1963   "The more total view, relationships among men and women of the
            upper middle class." Marriage and Family Living 25:140–45.
1965   The Significant Americans. New York: Appleton-Century-Crofts.
Cumming, Elaine
1969   "The multigenerational family and the crisis of widowhood." In
            Wilma Donahue et al. (eds.), Living in the Multigenerational Fam-
            ily. Ann Arbor, Mich.: University of Michigan Institute of Geron-
            tology.
Cumming, Elaine, Lois R. Dean, D. Newell, and Isabel McCaffrey
1960   "Disengagement—a tentative theory of aging." Sociometry
            23:23–35.
Cumming, Elaine and William Henry
1961   Growing Old. New York: Basic Books.
Cumming, Elaine and David M. Schneider
1961   "Sibling solidarity: A property of American kinship." American
            Anthropologist 63:498–507.
Cutter, Beverly R. and William G. Dyer
1965   "Initial adjustment processes in young married couples." Social
            Forces 44:195–201.
Darnley, Fred, Jr.
1975   "Adjustment to retirement: Integrity or despair." The Family
            Coordinator 24(2):217–26.
Datan, Nancy and Dean Rodeheaver
1977   "The sensuous grandmother." Paper presented at American Psy-
            chological Association meeting, San Francisco.

DeFrain, John
1977   "Support systems for family androgyny: Parents outline their needs." Paper presented at the National Council on Family Relations, San Diego, California.
Dentler, Robert A. and Peter Pineo
1960   "Marital adjustment and personal growth of husbands: A panel analysis." Marriage and Family Living 22:45–48.
Deutscher, Irwin
1962   "Socialization of postparental life." In Arnold Rose (ed.), Human Behavior and Social Process. Boston: Houghton Mifflin.
1968   "The quality of postparental life." In Bernice L. Neugarten (ed.), Middle Age and Aging. Chicago: University of Chicago Press.
Donahue, Wilma, Joyce Kornbluh, and Lawrence Power (eds.)
1969   Living in the Multigenerational Family. Ann Arbor, Mich.: University of Michigan Institute of Gerontology.
Douvan, Elizabeth and J. Adelson
1966   The Adolescent Experience. New York: John Wiley & Sons.
Duvall, Evelyn Millis
1971   Family Development. 4th ed. Philadelphia: J. B. Lippincott.
1977   Family Development. 5th ed. Philadelphia: J. B. Lippincott.
Erikson, Erik
1959   "Identity and the life cycle: Selected papers." Psychological Issues, monograph no. 1.
Eschen, Caryn and Margaret Hellie Huyck
1975   "Women and hysterectomy." Paper presented at the 28th Annual Scientific Meetings of the Gerontological Society, Louisville, Kentucky, October 26–30.
Farber, Bernard
1966   Kinship and Family Organization. New York: John Wiley & Sons.
Feigenbaum, Eliott, Marjorie F. Lowenthal, and Mella L. Trier
1966   "Sexual attitudes in the elderly." Paper presented at the Gerontological Society, New York.
Feldman, Harold
1964   "Development of the husband-wife relationship." Preliminary report, Cornell Studies of Marital Development: Study in the Transition to Parenthood. Department of Child Development and Family Relationships. New York State College of Home Economics. Cornell University.
1969   "Parent and marriage: Myths and realities." Paper presented at Merrill-Palmer Conference on the Family, Detroit.
1977   Personal communication.
Feldman, Harold and Margaret Feldman
1975   "The family life cycle: Some suggestions for recycling." Journal of Marriage and the Family 37(2):277–84.
Fengler, Alfred P.
1975   "Attitudinal orientations of wives toward their husbands' retirement." International Journal of Aging and Human Development 6(2):149–52.

Field, Minna
1972   The Aged, the Family, and the Community. New York: Columbia University Press.
Fisher, Seymour and D. Mendell
1956   "The communication of neurotic patterns over two and three generations." Psychiatry 10:41–46.
Freeman, H.
1972   "The generation gap: Attitudes of students and of their parents." Journal of Counseling Psychology 10:441–47.
Gans, Herbert J.
1962   The Urban Villagers: Group and Class Life of Italian-Americans. New York: The Free Press.
Garigue, Phillippe
1962   La Vie Familiale des Canadiens Français. Montreal: Presses Universitaires.
Gibson, Geoffrey
1969   "Kinship interaction and conjugal role relations." Paper presented at Ohio Valley Sociological Society and Midwest Sociological Society Joint Meeting, Indianapolis.
1970   "Kinship interaction with parents, children and siblings." Paper presented at Midwest Sociological Society, St. Louis.
1972   "Kin family network: Overheralded structure in past conceptualizations of family functioning." Journal of Marriage and the Family 34(1):13–23.
Gibson, Geoffrey and Edward Ludwig
1968a   "Family structure in a disabled population." Journal of Marriage and the Family 30(1):54–63.
1968b   "Family structure, role demands, and social behavior." Paper presented at Ohio Valley Sociological Society Meetings, Detroit.
Gilford, Rosalie
1974   "Marital satisfaction in retirement." Los Angeles: Andrus Gerontology Center.
Gilford, Rosalie and Dean Black
1972   "The grandchild-grandparent dyad: Ritual or relationship?" Paper presented at Gerontological Society meeting, San Juan, Puerto Rico.
Glick, Ira O., Robert S. Weiss, and C. Murray Parkes
1974   The First Year of Bereavement. New York: John Wiley & Sons.
Glick, Paul C.
1977   "Updating the family life cycle." Journal of Marriage and the Family 39(1):5–13.
Glick, Paul C. and Robert Parke, Jr.
1965   "New approaches in studying the life cycle of the family." Demography 2:187–202.
Goldfarb, Alvin I.
1965   "Psychodynamics and the three-generational family." In Ethel Shanas and Gordon F. Streib (eds.), Social Structure and the Family: Generational Relations. Englewood Cliffs, N.J.: Prentice-Hall.

Goode, William J.
1963   World Revolution and Family Patterns. Glencoe: The Free Press.
Gray, Robert M. and Ted C. Smith
1960   "Effect of employment on sex differences in attitudes toward the
            parental family." Marriage and Family Living 22:36–38.
Gubrium, Jaber F.
1974   "Marital desolation and the evaluation of everyday life in old
            age." Journal of Marriage and the Family 36:107–13.
1975   "Being single in old age." International Journal of Aging and
            Human Development 6:29–41.
Gurin, Gerald, Joseph Veroff, and Sheila Feld
1960   Americans View Their Mental Health: A National Interview
            Study. New York: Basic Books.
Hagestad, Gunnhild O.
1977   "Role change in adulthood: The transition to the empty nest."
            Unpublished manuscript, Committee on Human Development,
            University of Chicago.
Harris, Louis
1965   "Thoughts of loneliness haunt elderly Americans." Washington
            Post, November 29.
Harris, Louis and Associates
1975   The Myth and Reality of Aging in America. Washington, D.C.:
            National Council on the Aging.
Harvey, Carol D. and Howard M. Bahr
1974   "Widowhood, morale and affiliation." Journal of Marriage and the
            Family 36:97–106.
Hauser, Philip M.
1976   "Aging and world-wide population change. In Robert Binstock
            and Ethel Shanas (eds.), Handbook of Aging and the Social Sci-
            ences. New York: Van Nostrand Reinhold.
Havighurst, Robert
1957   "The social competence of middle aged people." Genetic Psycho-
            logical Monographs 56:297–395.
Havighurst, Robert, M. A. Munnicks, Thomas Joep, and B. L. Neugarten
1969   Adjustment to Retirement. A Cross-National Study. Assen,
            Netherlands: Van Goscum.
Hawkinson, William
1965   "Wish expectancy and practice in the interaction of generations."
            In Arnold Rose and Warren Peterson (eds.), Older People and
            Their Social World. Philadelphia: F. A. Davis.
Hayes, Maggie Parks and Nick Stinnett
1971   "Life satisfaction of middle-aged husbands and wives." Journal of
            Home Economics 63(9)669–74.
Hays, William C.
1977   "Theorists and theoretical frameworks identified by family
            sociologists." Journal of Marriage and the Family 39(1):59–65.
Hays, William C. and Charles H. Mindel
1973   "Extended kinship relations in black and white families." Journal
            of Marriage and the Family 35(1):51–57.

Hedden, L. J.
1974   "Intergenerational living: University dormitories." The Geron-
           tologist 14:283–85.
Henry, Jules
1951   "Family structure and the transmission of neurotic behavior."
           American Journal of Orthopsychiatry 21:800–18.
Henry, William E.
1964   "The theory of intrinsic disengagement." In P. From Hansen
           (ed.), Age with a Future. Copenhagen: Munksgaard.
Hess, Robert and Gerald Handel
1959   Family Worlds. Chicago: University of Chicago Press.
Heyman, Dorothy and Frances C. Jeffers
1968   "Wives and retirement: A pilot study." Journal of Gerontology
           23:488–96.
Hill, Reuben
1965   "Decision making and the family life cycle." In Ethel Shanas and
           Gordon F. Streib (eds.), Social Structure and the Family. En-
           glewood Cliffs, N.J.: Prentice-Hall.
Hill, Reuben, Nelson Foote, Joan Aldous, Robert Carlson, and Robert Mac-
Donald
1970   Family Development in Three Generations. Cambridge, Mass.:
           Schenkman.
Hill, Reuben and Donald A. Hansen
1960   "The identification of conceptual frameworks utilized in family
           study." Marriage and Family Living 22:299–311.
Hill, Reuben and R. H. Rodgers
1964   "The developmental approach." In Harold T. Christensen (ed.),
           Handbook of Marriage and the Family. Chicago: Rand McNally.
Hochschild, Arlie R.
1973   "A review of sex-role research." American Journal of Sociology
           78(4):1011–29.
1975   "Disengagement theory: A critique and proposal." American
           Sociological Review 40(5):553–69.
Hoffman, Lois Vladis
1978   "A cross-national study of early parent-child relations." In
           Richard Lerner and Graham Spanier (eds.), Child Influences on
           Marital and Family Interaction: A Life-Span Perspective. New
           York: Academic Press.
Hutchison, Ira W., III
1975   "The significance of marital status for morale and life satisfaction
           among lower-income elderly." Journal of Marriage and the Family
           37(2):287–93.
Huyck, Margaret Hellie
1977   "Sex and the older woman." In Lillian Troll, Joan Israel, and
           Kenneth Israel (eds.), Looking Ahead: A Woman's Guide to the
           Problems and Joys of Growing Older. Englewood Cliffs, N.J.:
           Prentice-Hall.
Ingraham, Mark H.
1974   My Purpose Holds: Reaction and Experiences in Retirement of

TIAA-CREF Annuitants. New York: Teachers Insurance and Annuity Assn./College Retirement Equities Fund.

Irish, Donald P.
1964   "Sibling interaction: A neglected aspect in family life research." Social Forces 42:279–88.

Jackson, Jacquelyne J.
1971   "Sex and social class variations in black aged parent-adult child relationships." Aging and Human Development 2:96–107.
1972a   "Marital life among aging blacks." The Family Coordinator 21(1):21–27.
1972b   "Social impacts of housing relocation upon urban, low-income black aged." The Gerontologist 12:32–37.
1977   "Older black women." In Lillian Troll, Joan Israel, and Kenneth Israel (eds.), Looking Ahead: A Woman's Guide to the Problems and Joys of Growing Older. Englewood Cliffs, N.J.: Prentice-Hall.

Jitodai, Ted T.
1963   "Migration and kinship contacts." Pacific Sociological Review 6:49–55.

Johnson, Elizabeth S. and Barbara J. Bursk
1977   "Relationships between the elderly and their adult children." The Gerontologist 17(1):90–96.

Kahana, Boaz and Eva Kahana
1970   "Grandparenthood from the perspective of the developing grandchild." Developmental Psychology 3(1):98–105.

Kahana, Eva and Boaz Kahana
1971   "Theoretical and research perspectives on grandparenthood." Aging and Human Development 2:261–68.

Kahana, Ralph J. and Sidney Levin
1971   "Aging and the conflict of generations." Journal of Geriatric Psychiatry 4(2):115–35.

Kalish, Richard A.
1972   "Of social values and the dying: A defense of disengagement." The Family Coordinator 21(1):81–94.
1976   "Death and dying in a social context." In Robert Binstock and Ethel Shanas (eds.), Handbook of Aging and the Social Sciences. New York: Van Nostrand Reinhold.

Kandel, Denise and Gerald Lesser
1972   Youth in Two Worlds. San Francisco: Jossey-Bass.

Karcher, C. J. and L. L. Linden
1975   "Family rejection of the aged and nursing home utilization." International Journal of Aging and Human Development 5:231–44.

Kelly, Burton
1966   "Congruency of self and mate perceptions as related to marital adjustment: A longitudinal study." Unpublished Ph.D. dissertation, University of Chicago.

Kent, Donald P. and Margaret B. Matson
1972   "The impact of health on the aged family." The Family Coordinator 21(1):29–36.

Kerckhoff, Alan C.
1964   "Husband-wife expectations and reactions to retirement." Journal

of Gerontology 19:510–16.

1965 "Nuclear and extended family relationships: A normative and behavioral analysis." In Ethel Shanas and Gordon F. Streib (eds.), Social Structure and the Family: Generational Relations. Englewood Cliffs, N.J.: Prentice-Hall.

1966a "Family and retirement." In Ida H. Simpson and John C. KcKinney (eds.), Social Aspects of Aging. Durham, N.C.: Duke University Press.

1966b "Norm-value clusters and the strain toward consistency among older married couples." In Ida H. Simpson and John C. McKinney (eds.), Social Aspects of Aging. Durham, N.C.: Duke University Press.

Kinsey, A. C., W. B. Pomeroy, and C. E. Martin
1948 Sexual Behavior in the Human Male. Philadelphia: W. B. Saunders.

Kinsey, A. C., W. B. Pomeroy, C. E. Martin, and P. H. Gebhard
1953 Sexual Behavior in the Human Female. Philadelphia: W. B. Saunders.

Klatsky, Sheila R.
1972 Patterns of Contact with Relatives. The Arnold and Caroline Rose Monograph Series in Sociology. Washington, D.C.: American Sociological Association.

Kohlberg, Lawrence
1973 "Continuities in childhood and adult moral development revisited." In Paul Baltes and K. Warner Schaie (eds.), Life-Span Development Psychology: Personality and Socialization. New York: Academic Press.

Komarovsky, Mirra
1964 Blue-Collar Marriage. New York: Random House.

Krasner, Jack D.
1969 "The reaction of the adult child to the institutionalization of the aged parent." In Wilma Donahue et al. (eds.), Living in the Multigenerational Family. Ann Arbor, Mich.: University of Michigan Institute of Gerontology.

Kreps, Juanita M.
1965 "The economics of intergenerational relationships." In Ethel Shanas and Gordon F. Streib (eds.), Social Structure and the Family: Generational Relations. Englewood Cliffs, N.J.: Prentice-Hall.

Kutner, Bernard
1956 Five Hundred over Sixty: A Community Survey of Aging. New York: Russell Sage Foundation.

Laws, Judith Long
1971 "A feminist review of the marital adjustment literature: the rape of the Locke." Journal of Marriage and the Family 33(3):483–516.

Lawton, M. Powell, and B. Simon
1968 "The ecology of social relationships in housing for the elderly." The Gerontologist 8:108–15.

Leach, Jean M.
1964 "The intergenerational approach in casework with the aging." Social Casework 45(3):144–49.

Lee, Anne S.
1974   "Return migration in the United States." International Migration Review 8:283–300.
Leichter, Hope and William E. Mitchell
1967   Kinship and Casework. New York: Russell Sage Foundation.
LeMasters, E. E.
1957   "Parenthood as crisis." Marriage and Family Living 19:352–55.
LeVine, Robert A.
1965   "Intergenerational tensions and extended family structure in Africa." In Ethel Shanas and Gordon F. Streib (eds.), Social Structure and the Family: Generational Relations. Englewood Cliffs, N.J.: Prentice-Hall.

Lipman, Aaron
1960   "Marital roles of the retired aged." Merrill-Palmer Quarterly of Behavior and Development 6:192–95.
1961   "Role conceptions and morale of couples in retirement." Journal of Gerontology 16:267–71.
1962   "Role conceptions of couples in retirement." In Clark Tibbitts and Wilma Donahue (eds.), Social and Psychological Aspects of Aging. New York: Columbia University Press.
Litman, Theodor J.
1971   "Health care and the family: A three-generational analysis." Medical Care 9:67–81.
Litwak, Eugene
1960a   "Occupational mobility and extended family cohesion." American Sociological Review 25:9–21.
1960b   "Geographic mobility and extended family cohesion." American Sociological Review 25:385–94.
1960c   "The use of extended family groups in the achievement of social goals." Social Problems 7:177–87.
1965   "Extended kin relations in an industrial democratic society." In Ethel Shanas and Gordon Streib (eds.), Social Structure and the Family: Generational Relations. Englewood Cliffs, N.J.: Prentice-Hall.

Litwak, Eugene and Ivan Szelenyi
1969   "Primary group structures and their functions: Kin, neighbors, and friends." American Sociological Review 34(4):465–81.
Lobsenz, Norman M.
1974   "Sex and the senior citizen." New York Times Magazine, January 20.
Lopata, Helena Z.
1960   "The life cycle of the social role of housewife." Sociology and Social Research 51(1):5–22.
1969   "Role changes in widowhood." Dittoed paper.
1971a   "Widows as a minority group." The Gerontologist 11(1, part 2):67–77.
1971b   Occupation: Housewife. New York: Oxford University Press.
1973   Widowhood in an American City. Cambridge, Mass.: Schenkman.

1977   "The meaning of friendship in widowhood." In Lillian Troll, Joan Israel, and Kenneth Israel (eds.), Looking Ahead: A Woman's Guide to the Problems and Joys of Growing Older. Englewood Cliffs, N.J.: Prentice-Hall.

Lowenthal, Marjorie F.
1977   "Toward a sociopsychological theory of change in adulthood and old age." In James Birren and K. Warner Schaie (eds.), Handbook of the Psychology of Aging. New York: Van Nostrand Reinhold.

Lowenthal, Marjorie F. and D. Chiriboga
1972   "Transition to the empty nest: Crisis, challenge, or relief?" Archives of General Psychiatry 26:8–14.

Lowenthal, Marjorie F. and Clayton Havens
1968   "Interaction and adaptation: Intimacy as a critical variable." American Sociological Review 33:20–31.

Lowenthal, Marjorie F., Majda Thurnher, David Chiriboga, and Associates
1975   Four Stages of Life. San Francisco: Jossey-Bass.

Lozier, J. and R. Althouse
1974   "Special enforcement of behavior toward elders in an Appalachian mountain settlement." The Gerontologist 14:69–80.

Lurie, Elinore E.
1974   "Sex and stage differences in perceptions of marital and family relationships." Journal of Marriage and the Family 36(2):260–69.

Maas, Henry S. and Joseph A. Kuypers
1974   From Thirty to Seventy. San Francisco: Jossey-Bass.

MacIver, Robert M. and Charles H. Page
1949   Sociology: An Introductory Analysis. New York: Rinehart.

McKain, Walter C., Jr.
1969   Retirement Marriage. Storrs, Conn.: University of Connecticut Agriculture Experiment Station.
1972   "A new look at older marriages." The Family Coordinator 21(1):61–70.

Maddison, David and Agnes Viola
1968   "The health of widows in the year following bereavement." Journal of Psychosomatic Research 12:297–306.

Maddox, George L.
1968   "Persistence of life style among the elderly: A longitudinal study of patterns of social activity in relation to life satisfaction." In B. Neugarten (ed.), Middle Age and Aging. Chicago: University of Chicago Press.

Mannheim, Karl
1952   "The problem of generations." In Paul Kecskemeti (ed.), Essays in the Sociology of Knowledge. London: Routledge and Kegan Paul.

Marris, Peter
1961   Family and Social Change in an African City: A Study of Rehousing in Lagos. London: Routledge and Kegan Paul.

Martel, Martin and W. W. Morris
1960   Life after Sixty in Iowa. Iowa City: Institute of Gerontology.

Masters, William H. and Virginia Johnson
1966   Human Sexual Response. Boston: Little, Brown.
1968   "Human sexual response: The aging female and the aging male."
          In B. Neugarten (ed.), Middle Age and Aging. Chicago: Univer-
          sity of Chicago Press.
Meddin, Jay
1975   "Generations and aging: A longitudinal study." International
          Journal of Aging and Human Development 6(2):85–101.
Miller, Sheila J.
1972   "The influence of extended family orientations and economic aspi-
          rations on the decision to migrate." Unpublished doctoral disserta-
          tion, University of Kansas, Lawrence.
1973   "Family life cycle, extended family orientations, and economic
          aspirations as factors in family migration." Paper presented at the
          Population Association of America annual meeting. Abstract in
          Population Index 39(3):326.
1976   "Family life cycle, extended family orientations, and economic
          aspirations as factors in the propensity to migrate." Sociological
          Quarterly 17:323–35.
1977   "Widowhood and the older woman." In Symposium on Economic
          Resources of Older Women. Paper presented at the annual meet-
          ing of the Gerontological Society, San Francisco.
1978   "Will the real 'older woman' please stand up?" In Mildred M.
          Seltzer, Sherry L. Corbett, and Robert C. Atchley (eds.), Social
          Problems of the Aging: Readings. Belmont, Ca.: Wadsworth.
Moberg, David O.
1972   "Religion and the aging family." The Family Coordinator
          29(1):47–60.
Montgomery, James E.
1972   "The housing patterns of older families." The Family Coordinator
          21:37–46.
Morgan, Mildred I.
1969   "The middle life and the aging family." The Family Coordinator
          18:296–98.
Murray, Janet
1973   "Family structure in the preretirement years." Social Security
          Bulletin 36:24–45.
1976   "Family structure in the preretirement years." In Almost 65:
          Baseline Data from the Retirement History Study. Washington,
          D.C.: U.S. Department of Health, Education, and Welfare.
Murstein, B. I.
1961   "The complementary need hypothesis in newlyweds and middle
          aged married couples." Journal of Abnormal and Social Psychol-
          ogy 63:194–97.
National Center for Health Statistics
1974   Vital Statistics of the United States, 1970. Vol. 3, Marriage and
          Divorce. Washington, D.C.: U.S. Government Printing Office.
Nesselroade, John R., K. Warner Schaie, and Paul Baltes
1972   "Ontogenetic and generational components of structural and quan-
          titative change in adult cognitive behavior." Journal of Gerontol-
          ogy 27:222–28.

Neubeck, Gerhard (ed.)
1969   Extramarital Relations. Englewood Cliffs, N.J.: Prentice-Hall.
Neugarten, Bernice L.
1968   Middle Age and Aging. Chicago: University of Chicago Press.
Neugarten, Bernice L. and David Gutmann
1968   "Age-sex roles and personality in middle age. A thematic apper-
            ception study." In Bernice Neugarten and Associates (eds.), Per-
            sonality in Middle and Late Life. New York: Atherton.
Neugarten, Bernice L., Robert Havighurst, and Sheldon Tobin
1968   "Personality and patterns of aging." In Bernice Neugarten (ed.),
            Middle Age and Aging. Chicago: University of Chicago Press.
Neugarten, Bernice L. and Karol K. Weinstein
1964   "The changing American grandparent." Journal of Marriage and
            the Family 26:199–204.
Neugarten, Bernice L., Vivian Wood, Ruth Kraines, and Barbara Loomis
1963   "Women's attitudes toward the menopause." Vita Humana
            6:110–51.
New York Times
1975   "More executives refusing to relocate," November 7, p. 11.
Nowak, Carol
1975   "The appearance signal in adult development." Unpublished doc-
            toral dissertation, Wayne State University, Detroit.
Nye, F. Ivan and Felix M. Berardo
1973a   "Death and the widowed family." In Kenneth J. Scott (ed.), The
            Family: Its Structure and Interaction. New York: Macmillan.
1973b   "The retired family." In Kenneth J. Scott (ed.), The Family: Its
            Structure and Interaction. New York: Macmillan.
Orthner, Dennis K.
1975   "Leisure activity patterns and marital satisfaction over the marital
            career." Journal of Marriage and the Family 37:91–102.
Parkes, C. Murray
1972   Bereavement. New York: International Universities Press.
Parkes, C. Murray, R. Benjamin, and R. A. Fitzgerald
1969   "Broken heart: A statistical study of increased mortality among
            widowers." British Medical Journal 1:740–43.
Parron, Eugenia
1978   "An exploratory study of intimacy in golden wedding couples."
            Unpublished master's thesis, Rutgers University.
Parsons, Talcott
1965   "The normal American family." In Seymour Farber, Piero Mus-
            tacchi, and Roger H. Wilson (eds.), Man and Civilization: The
            Family's Search for Survival. New York: McGraw-Hill.
Petrowsky, Marc
1976   "Marital status, sex, and the social networks of the elderly."
            Journal of Marriage and the Family 38(3):749–56.
Pfeiffer, Eric, Adriaan Verwoerdt, and Hsiah-Shan Wang
1968   "Sexual behavior in aged men and women." Archives of General
            Psychiatry 19:756–58.
Pihlblad, C. Terence and Robert L. McNamara
1965   "Social adjustment of elderly people in three small towns." In

Arnold M. Rose and Warren A. Peterson (eds.), Older People and Their Social World. Philadelphia: F.A. Davis.

Pineo, Peter
1961   "Disenchantment in the later years of marriage." Marriage and Family Living 23:3–11.
1968   "Disenchantment in the later years of marriage." In Bernice Neugarten (ed.), Middle Age and Aging. Chicago: University of Chicago Press.

Pope, H.
1964   "Economic deprivation and social participation in a group of 'middle class' factory workers." Social Problems 11:290–300.

Powers, Edward A.
1971   "The effect of the wife's employment on household tasks among postparental couples; a research note." Aging and Human Development 2:284–87.

Powers, Edward A. and Gordon L. Bultena
1976   "Sex differences in intimate friendships of old age." Journal of Marriage and the Family 38(4):739–47.

Powers, Edward A., Patricia Keith, and Willis H. Goudy
1975   "Family relationships and friendships." In Robert C. Atchley (ed.), Environments and the Rural Aged. Washington, D.C.: Gerontological Society.

Reedy, Margaret N.
1977   "Age and sex differences in personal needs and the nature of love: A study of happily married young, middle-aged, and older adult couples." Unpublished doctoral dissertation, University of Southern California, Los Angeles.

Reiss, Paul J.
1962   "Extended kinship system: Correlates of and attitudes on frequency of interaction." Marriage and Family Living 24:333–39.

Rheinstein, Max
1960   "Duty of children to support parents." In E. W. Burgess (ed.), Aging in Western Societies. Chicago: University of Chicago Press.

Rieger, Jon H.
1972   "Geographic mobility and the occupational attainment of rural youth: A longitudinal evaluation." Rural Sociology 37:189–207.

Riley, Lawrence E. and Elmer A. Spreitzer
1974   "A model for the analysis of lifetime marriage patterns." Journal of Marriage and the Family 36(1):64–70.

Riley, Matilda and Anne Foner
1968   Aging and Society. Vol. 1, An Inventory of Research Findings. New York: Russell Sage Foundation.

Robbins, Ira S.
1971   Housing the Elderly: Background and Issues. Washington, D.C.: White House Conference on Aging.

Roberts, William L. and Ann E. Roberts
1975   "Factors in lifestyles of couples married over 50 years." Washington, D.C.: Gerontological Society.

Robertson, Joan F.
1975   "Interaction in three generation families, parents as mediators:
            Toward a theoretical perspective." International Journal of Aging
            and Human Development 6(2):103–10.
1976   "Significance of grandparents—perceptions of young adult grand-
            children." The Gerontologist 16(2):137–40.
1977   "Grandmotherhood: A study of role conceptions." Journal of
            Marriage and the Family 39(1):165–74.
Robins, Lee N. and Miroda Tomanec
1962   "Closeness to blood relatives outside the immediate family." Mar-
            riage and Family Living 24:340–46.
Rodgers, Roy H.
1964   "Toward a theory of family development." Journal of Marriage
            and the Family 26:262–70.
Rogers, Everett and Hans Sebald
1962   "A distinction between familism, family integration and kinship
            orientation." Marriage and Family Living 24:25–30.
Rollins, Boyd C. and Kenneth L. Cannon
1974   "Marital satisfaction over the family life cycle: A re-evaluation."
            Journal of Marriage and the Family 35:271–82.
Rollins, Boyd C. and Harold Feldman
1970   "Marital satisfaction over the family life cycle." Journal of Mar-
            riage and the Family 32:20–28.
Rose, Arnold M. and Warren A. Peterson
1965   Older People and Their Social World. Philadelphia: F. A. Davis.
Rosenberg, George S.
1968   "Age, poverty and isolation from friends in the urban working
            class." Journal of Gerontology 23:533–38.
1970   The Worker Grows Old. San Francisco: Jossey-Bass.
Rosenberg, George S. and Donald F. Anspach
1973   "Sibling solidarity in the working class." Journal of Marriage and
            the Family 35(1):108–13.
Rosenheim, Margaret K.
1965   "Social welfare and its implications for family living." In Ethel
            Shanas and Gordon F. Streib (eds.), Social Structure and the Fam-
            ily: Generational Relations. Englewood Cliffs, N.J.: Prentice-
            Hall.
Rosow, Irving
1962   "Old age: One moral dilemma of an affluent society." The Geron-
            tologist 2:182–91.
1964   "Local concentrations of aged and intergenerational friendships."
            In P. From Hansen (ed.), Age with a Future. Copenhagen:
            Munksgaard.
1965a   "Relationship of older persons to family and friends." Welfare in
            Review 3(7):17.
1965b   "Intergenerational relationships: Problems and proposals." In
            Ethel Shanas and Gordon Streib (eds.), Social Structure and the
            Family: Generational Relations. Englewood Cliffs, N.J.:
            Prentice-Hall.

1965c   "The aged, family and friends." Social Security Bulletin 28(11):18–20.

1967   Social Integration of the Aged. New York: The Free Press.

Rubenstein, Daniel I.

1971   "An examination of social participation found among a national sample of black and white elderly." Aging and Human Development 2:172–88.

Rubin, Isadore

1965   Sexual Life after Sixty. New York: Basic Books.

1968   "The 'sexless older years'—a socially harmful stereotype." Annals of the American Academy of Political and Social Sciences 376:86–95.

Rubin, L. B.

1975   Worlds of Pain. New York: Basic Books.

Ryder, Robert G.

1968   "Husband-wife dyads versus married strangers." Family Process 7:233–38.

Ryder, Robert G. and D. W. Goodrich

1966   "Married couples' responses to disagreement." Family Process 5:30–42.

Saltz, Rosalyn

1970   "Evaluation of a foster grandparent program." In A. Kalushin (ed.), Child Welfare Services: A Sourcebook. New York: Macmillan.

Savitsky, E. and H. Sharkey

1972   "The geriatric patient and his family." Journal of Geriatric Psychiatry 5:3–19.

Schaie, K. Warner

1967   "Age changes and age differences." The Gerontologist 1(Part 1):128–32.

Schlein, John

1962   "Mother-in-law: A problem in kinship terminology." ETC 19:161–71.

Schneider, David

1968   American Kinship. Englewood Cliffs, N.J.: Prentice-Hall.

Schoen, R. and V. E. Nelson

1974   "Marriage, divorce and mortality; a life table analysis." Demography 11:267–90.

Schorr, Alvin L.

1960   Filial Responsibility in the Modern American Family. Washington, D.C.: Social Security Administration.

1962   "Filial responsibility and the aging, or beyond pluck and luck." Social Security Bulletin 25(5):4–9.

Schulman, Norman

1975   "Life cycle variation in patterns of close relationships." Journal of Marriage and the Family 37(4):813–21.

Schwarzweller, Harry K.

1964   "Parental family ties and social integration of rural to urban migrants." Journal of Marriage and the Family 26:410–16.

Schwarzweller, Harry K. and John F. Seggar
1967   "Kinship involvement: A factor in the adjustment of rural mig-
            rants." Journal of Marriage and the Family 29:662–71.
Scott, Frances G.
1962   "Family group structure and patterns of social interaction."
            American Journal of Sociology 68:214–28.
Shanas, Ethel
1960   "Family responsibility and the health of older people." Journal of
            Gerontology 15:408–11.
1961   "Living arrangements of older people in the United States." The
            Gerontologist 1:27–29.
1962   The Health of Older People: A Social Survey. Cambridge, Mass.:
            Harvard University Press.
1964   "Family and household characteristics of older people in the
            United States." In P. From Hansen (ed.), Age with a Future.
            Copenhagen: Munksgaard.
1967   "Family help patterns and social class in three countries." Journal
            of Marriage and the Family 29:257–66.
1968   "A note on restriction of life space: Attitudes of age cohorts."
            Journal of Health and Social Behavior 9:86–90.
1973   "Family-kin networks and aging in cross-cultural perspective."
            Journal of Marriage and the Family 35(3):505–11.

Shanas, Ethel, Peter Townsend, Dorothy Wedderburn, Henning Friis, Poul
Milhhøj, and Jan Stehouver
1968   Older People in Three Industrial Societies. New York: Atherton
            Press.
Shelton, Austin J.
1969   "Igbo child-rearing, eldership, and dependence: A comparison of
            two cultures." In Richard Kalish (ed.), The Dependencies of Old
            People. Ann Arbor, Mich.: University of Michigan Institute of
            Gerontology.
Sherman, Sanford N.
1961   "The concept of the family in casework theory." In Nathan Ac-
            kerman (ed.), Exploring the Base for Family Therapy. New York:
            Family Service Association of America.
Shock, Nathan W. (ed.)
1950   A Classified Bibliography of Gerontology and Geriatrics. Supple-
            ment. Stanford, California: Stanford University Press. (Also 1955
            and 1961.)
Silverman, Phyllis R.
1972   "Widowhood and preventive intervention." The Family Coor-
            dinator 21(1):95–102.
Simpson, Ida H. and John C. McKinney (eds.)
1966   Social Aspects of Aging. Durham, N.C.: Duke University Press.
Smelser, Neil J.
1966   "The modernization of social relations." In Myron Weiner (ed.),
            Modernization: The Dynamics of Growth. New York: Basic
            Books.

Smith, Harold E.
1965   "Family interaction patterns of the aged: A review." In Arnold
            M. Rose and Warren A. Peterson (eds.), Older People and Their
            Social World. Philadelphia: F. A. Davis.
Smith, Joel
1966   "The narrowing social world of the aged." In Ida H. Simpson and
            John C. McKinney (eds.), Social Aspects of Aging. Durham,
            N.C.: Duke University Press.
Snyder, Paul Wayne
1972   "The effect of new marriages among the aged upon the disen-
            gagement process." Dissertation Abstracts International
            32(A):7101–A, May–June.
Somerville, Rose M.
1972   "The future of family relationships in the middle and older years:
            Clues in fiction." The Family Coordinator 21:487–98.
Soyer, David
1972   "The geriatric patient and his family: Helping the family to live
            with itself." Journal of Geriatric Psychiatry 5(1):52–65.
Spanier, Graham B., Robert A. Lewis, and Charles L. Coles
1975   "Marital adjustment over the family life cycle: The issue of cur-
            vilinearity." Journal of Marriage and the Family 37:263–75.
Speck, Ross V. and Uri Rueveni
1969   "Network therapy—a developing concept." Family Process
            8(2):182–91.
Spence, Donald and Thomas Lonner
1971   "The 'empty nest': A transition within motherhood." The Family
            Coordinator 20:369–75.
Stehouwer, Jan
1965   "Relations between generations and the three-generation house-
            hold in Denmark." In Ethel Shanas and Gordon F. Streib (eds.),
            Social Structure and the Family. Englewood Cliffs, N.J.:
            Prentice-Hall.
Stephens, J.
1974   "Romance in the SRO; relationships of elderly men and women in
            a slum hotel." The Gerontologist 14:279–82.
Stinnett, Nick, Linda M. Carter, and James E. Montgomery
1972   "Older persons' perceptions of their marriages." Journal of Mar-
            riage and the Family 34:665–70.
Stinnett, Nick, Janet Collins, and James E. Montgomery
1970   "Marital need satisfaction of older husbands and wives." Journal
            of Marriage and the Family 32(3):428–34.
Streib, Gordon F.
1958   "Family patterns in retirement." Journal of Social Issues 24:46–
            60.
1965   "Intergenerational relations: Perspectives of the two generations
            on the older parent." Journal of Marriage and the Family 27:469–
            76.
1972   "Older families and their troubles: Familial and social responses."
            The Family Coordinator 21(1):5–20.

Streib, Gordon F. and Clement J. Schneider
1971   Retirement in American Society. Ithaca, N.Y.: Cornell University Press.

Streib, Gordon F. and Wayne Thompson
1960   "The older person in a family context." In Clark Tibbetts (ed.), Handbook of Social Gerontology. Chicago: University of Chicago Press.

Stryker, Sheldon
1964   "The interactional and situational approaches." In Harold T. Christensen (ed.), Handbook of Marriage and the Family. Chicago: Rand McNally.

Stuchert, Robert P.
1963   "Occupational mobility and family relationships." Social Forces 41:301–7.

Sussman, Marvin B.
1955   "Activity patterns of post-parental couples and their relationship to family continuity." Marriage and Family Living 17:338–41.
1960   "Intergenerational family relationships and social role changes in middle age." Journal of Gerontology 15(1):71–75.
1965   "Relationships of adult children with their parents in the United States." In Ethel Shanas and Gordon F. Streib (eds.), Social Structure and the Family: Generational Relations. Englewood Cliffs, N.J.: Prentice-Hall.
1968a   "Current state and perspectives of research in the family." Social Science Information 7(3):35–52.
1968b   Sourcebook in Marriage and the Family, 3rd ed. Boston: Houghton Mifflin.

Sussman, Marvin B. and Lee Burchinal
1962a   "Parental aid to married children: Implications for family functioning." Marriage and Family Living 24:320–32.
1962b   "Kin family network: Unheralded structure in current conceptualizations of family functioning." Marriage and Family Living 24:231–40.

Suzuki, Peter T.
1975   "Minority group aged in America: A comprehensive bibliography of recent publications on blacks, Mexican-Americans, native Americans, Chinese, and Japanese." Council of Planning Librarians, Exchange Bibliography #816:1–25.

Sweetser, Dorrian Apple
1963   "Asymmetry in intergenerational family relationships." Social Forces 41:346–52.

Taylor, P. H.
1964   "Role and role conflicts in a group of middle class wives and mothers." Sociological Review 21(3):317–27.

Thompson, Wayne E. and Gordon Streib
1961   "Meaningful activity in a family context." In R. W. Kleemeier (ed.), Aging and Leisure: A Research Perspective into the Meaningful Use of Time. New York: Oxford University Press.

Tibbetts, Clark
1960   Handbook of Social Gerontology. Chicago: University of Chicago Press.
Townsend, Peter
1957   The Family Life of Old People: An Inquiry in East London. Glencoe, Ill.: The Free Press.
1965   "The effects of family structure on the likelihood of admission to an institution in old age: The application of a general theory." In Ethel Shanas and Gordon F. Streib (eds.), Social Structure and the Family: Generational Relations. Englewood Cliffs, N.J.: Prentice-Hall.
1968   "The emergence of the four-generation family in industrial society." In Bernice Neugarten (ed.), Middle Age and Aging. Chicago: University of Chicago Press.
Treas, Judith and Anke VanHilst
1976   "Marriage and remarriage rates among older Americans." The Gerontologist 16(2):132–36.
Troll, Lillian
1969a   "Approval of spouse in middle age." Proceedings, American Psychological Association.
1969b   "Issues in the study of the family." (Review of The Psycho-social Interior of the Family, edited by Gerald Handel. Chicago: Aldine, 1967.) Merrill-Palmer Quarterly of Behavior and Development 15(2):221–26.
1970   "Issues in the study of generations." Aging and Human Development 1:199–218.
1971a   "The family of later life: A decade review." Journal of Marriage and the Family 33:263–90.
1971b   "The generation gap in later life: An introductory discussion and some preliminary findings." Sociological Focus 5(1):18–28.
1972a   "Is parent-child conflict what we mean by the generation gap?" The Family Coordinator 21:347–49.
1972b   "The salience of members of three generation families for one another." Paper presented at American Psychological Association Meeting, Honolulu, September.
1973   "The onus of 'developmental tasks' and other reactions to Duvall's Family Development in its fourth edition." International Journal of Aging and Human Development 4(1):67–73.
1975   Early and Middle Adulthood. Monterey, Ca.: Brooks/Cole.
Troll, Lillian and Vern Bengtson
1978   "Generations in the family." In Wesley Burr, Reuben Hill, Ivan Nye, and Ira L. Reiss (eds.), Contemporary Theories About the Family. New York: The Free Press.
Troll, Lillian, Joan Israel, and Kenneth Israel
1977   Looking Ahead: A Woman's Guide to the Problems and Joys of Growing Older. Englewood Cliffs, N.J.: Prentice-Hall.
Troll, Lillian, Bernice Neugarten, and Ruth Kraines
1969   "Similarities on values and other personality characteristics in col-

lege students and their parents." Merrill-Palmer Quarterly of Behavior and Development 15:323–37.

Troll, Lillian and Jean Smith
1976 "Attachment through the life span: Some questions about dyadic relations in later life. Human Development 3:156–71.

Troll, Lillian and Barbara Turner
1976 "The secular trends in sex roles and the family of later life." Paper presented at Ford Foundation conference, Merrill-Palmer Institute.

Turner, Joseph G.
1975 "Patterns of intergenerational exchange: a developmental approach." International Journal of Aging and Human Development 6(2):111–15.

Tyhurst, James S., Lee Salk, and Miriam Kennedy
1957 "Mortality, morbidity, and retirement." American Journal of Public Health 47:1434–44.

Uhlenberg, Peter
1974 "Cohort variations in family life cycle experiences of U.S. females." Journal of Marriage and the Family 36(2):284–92.

Updegraff, Sue G.
1968 "Changing role of the grandmother." Journal of Home Economics 60:177–80.

U.S. Bureau of the Census, U.S. Census of Population: 1960
1964 Subject Reports—Women by Number of Children Ever Born. Final Report PC (2)-3A. Washington, D.C.: U.S. Government Printing Office.
1966 Subject Reports—Marital Status. Final Report PC-4E. Washington, D.C.: U.S. Government Printing Office.
1975 Characteristics of the Low-Income Population: 1973. Current Population Reports Series P-60, No. 98. Washington, D.C.: U.S. Government Printing Office.
1976 Demographic Aspects of Aging and the Older Population in the United States. Current Population Reports: Special Studies Series P-23(59):46.

U.S. Department of Health, Education, and Welfare
1969 Adult Development and Aging Abstracts. Washington, D.C.: U.S. Department of Health, Education, and Welfare, Public Health Service, National Institutes of Health.

U.S. Department of Labor, Women's Bureau
1969 Handbook on Women Workers. Women's Bureau Bulletin 294. Washington, D.C.: U.S. Government Printing Office.

Veroff, Joseph and Sheila Feld
1970 Marriage and Work in America: A Study of Motives and Roles. New York: Van Nostrand Reinhold.

Verwoerdt, Adriaan, Eric Pfeiffer, and Hsiah-Shan Wang
1969 "Sexual behavior in senescence: Changes in sexual activity and interest in aging men and women." Journal of Geriatric Psychiatry 2:168–80.

Wake, Sandra Byford and Michael J. Sporakowski
1972   "An intergenerational comparison of attitudes towards supporting aged parents." Journal of Marriage and the Family 34:42–48.
Wales, Jeffrey B.
1974   "Sexuality in middle and old age: A critical review of the literature." Case Western Reserve Journal of Sociology 6:82–105.
Walker, K.
1970   "Time spent by husbands in household work." Family Economics Review, June, pp. 8–11.
Walters, Ellen R. and David F. Mitchell
1974   "Selected aspects of urban living among the transition area aged in comparative perspective." In Characteristics and Needs of the Population Living near the Greensboro Business District. Technical Report 13. Home Economics Center for Research, University of North Carolina, Greensboro.
Watson, J. Allen and Vira R. Kivett
1976   "Influences on the life satisfaction of older fathers." The Family Coordinator 25(4):482–88.
Weg, Ruth
1975   "Sexual changes." In Diana S. Woodruff and James E. Birren (eds.), Aging: Scientific and Social Issues. New York: D. Van Nostrand.
Westley, William and Nathan Epstein
1960   "Family structure and emotional health: A case study." Marriage and Family Living 22:25–27.
1961   Silent Majority. San Francisco: Jossey-Bass.
White House Conference on Aging
1971   Work Book on Housing. Washington, D.C.
Wilder, Charles S.
1971   "Chronic conditions and limitations of mobility: United States, July 1966 to June 1968." Vital and Health Statistics, series 10, no. 61.
Wilder, Mary H.
1972   "Home care for persons 55 years and over: United States, July 1966 to June 1968." Vital and Health Statistics, series 10, no. 73.
Wilkening, E. A., Joas Bosco Pinto, and Jose Pastore
1968   "Role of the extended family in migration and adaptation in Brazil." Marriage and Family Living 30:689–95.
Williams, Richard and Claudine Wirths
1965   Lives Through the Years. New York: Atherton Press.
Willmott, Peter and Michael Young
1960   Family and Class in a London Suburb. London: Routledge and Kegan Paul.
Winch, Robert F. and Scott A. Greer
1968   "Urbanism, ethnicity, and extended families." Marriage and Family Living 30:40–45.
Wood, Vivian and Joan F. Robertson
1976   "The significance of grandparenthood." In Jaber F. Gubrium

(ed.), Time, Roles, and Self in Old Age. New York: Human Science Press.

Youmans, E. Grant
1963   Aging Patterns in a Rural and Urban Area of Kentucky. Lexington, Ky.: University of Kentucky Agricultural Experiment Station.
1967a   "Family disengagement among older urban and rural women." Journal of Gerontology 22(2):209–11.
1967b   Older Rural Americans. Lexington, Ky.: University of Kentucky Press.

Young, Michael and Hildred Geertz
1961   "Old age in London and San Francisco." British Journal of Sociology 12:124–41.

Young, Michael and Peter Willmott
1957   Family and Kinship in East London. London: Routledge and Kegan Paul.

Index